Ghana Priorities

Analysing costs and benefits

About the Ghana Priorities Project

The project aims to promote social, economic and environmental benefit-cost analysis as decision support when choosing between various policy interventions. It was conducted in collaboration with the National Development Planning Commission using the Copenhagen Consensus Center's award-winning methodology.

The project unites the best academic research, employing cost-benefit analysis, with sector expert input, broad and inclusive stakeholder engagement, and extensive policy outreach, to evaluate and prioritise the smartest interventions.

For more information on the project, including the content of this book, please visit www.ghanapriorities.com

About National Development Planning Commission

Since its formation in 1993, the Commission has worked closely with every President under the Fourth Republic to prepare the Coordinated Programme of Economic and Social Development Policies, which the President is required by the Constitution to submit to Parliament within two years of assuming office. The Commission also led the process of preparing the country's first long-term (25-year) national development plan, Vision 2020.

About Copenhagen Consensus Center

The Copenhagen Consensus is an award-winning think tank that researches the smartest solutions for the world's biggest problems and has helped policy-makers and philanthropists how to spend their money most effectively. Copenhagen Consensus has helped to focus billions of dollars of global aid and development spending on smarter priorities. The world's oldest academic publisher, Cambridge University Press, has published seven volumes of the Center's research.

Ghana Priorities

Analysing costs and benefits

by

Bjorn Lomborg

Samuel Kobina Annim

Ralph Essem Nordjo

This work has been produced as a part of the Ghana Priorities Project, a collaboration between the National Development Planning Commission and the Copenhagen Consensus Center.

National Development Planning Commission

Republic of Ghana

COPENHAGEN CONSENSUS CENTER

Please cite the work as follows: Lomborg, Annim and Nordjo, Ghana Priorities - analysing costs and benefits, National Development Planning Commission and Copenhagen Consensus Center 2021.

Graphs and figures made with infogram.com, data source is the project research paper analysing the respective interventions.

Publisher information:

ISBN 978-1-940003-25-2

www.copenhagenconsensus.com

CONTENTS

Foreword

By Dr. Kodjo Esseim Mensah-Abrampa

No country, however prosperous, can do everything. That is why it is crucial that every cedi is spent in the best possible way yielding the best result for humanity.

In Ghana, the National Development Planning Commission (NDPC), among others coordinates the preparation of long and medium-term national development policy frameworks serving as the government's blueprint on national development. Such policy frameworks and plans are crucial for facilitating the decision on which policies should be funded and at what time.

It is for this reason that the NDPC working with its entire technical team, headed by the Director General, partnered with the award-winning international think tank Copenhagen Consensus Center to create the Ghana Priorities project. The goal was to create a wide-ranging and exciting knowledge base for Ghana on costs and benefits. This is indeed one of the main strategic tools for NDPC, to ensure that the institution provides evidence-based information to support decision makers — from politicians, through public officers, to voters — to identify and advocate for the policies that contribute the most to a prosperous Ghana.

The benefits from such this project are manifold, but the initiative particularly focuses on enhancing NDPCs approach of fostering both evidence-based information and growing the intellectual capital. We are already focusing on innovative technologies and approaches to enhance the quality of life and prosperity across all communities. The effort is to bring in high-quality skills and technologies to expedite and scale up interventions, across different sectors such as education, health, livelihoods, and more.

The process undertaken by Ghana Priorities is entirely aligned to this trajectory through a cutting edge analysis. It is particularly innovative to compare such a broad range of different spending options using cost-benefit analysis. Very few governments or organisations undertake such objective, choice enhancing work, because it is so complex. The Ghana Priority Project, applying this approach breaks new ground, by standardising the academic enquiry results and ensuring that the costs and benefits of various policies can are comprehensive and appreciated by key stakeholders.

The contribution that Ghana Priorities makes to enhancing intellectual capacity and strengthening the link between research and policy development is important and fundamental to NDPC's endeavour. Some of the finest economists and specialists from Ghana and across the region contributed academically to this project, bringing their own experienced-based perspectives to identifying the effect of proposed solutions on resources requirements and the social and economic fabric of the country.

Over the past one and half years, we have worked hard with 28 teams of economic experts from Ghana and abroad to study the costs and benefits of 79 concrete policy interventions to improve the future of the country. These analyses provided a foundation of knowledge. They were based on extensive peer-reviewed academic work within many important areas such as agriculture, education, health and infrastructure.

The studied enquired and revealed the worth of development benefits that can be achieved for each cedi spent in Ghana. The compendium has resulted in more than 1000 pages of research, much of which has been highlighted in more than 30 articles in the Daily Graphic and across the national media.

This compendium enhanced the environment for an inclusive and more informed debate on priorities across all sectors. It indicates policies where great benefits can be achieved at moderate cost, but it also reveals policies where even large expenditures will only achieve little gains. It is acknowledged that policy setting is not just about finding the biggest social returns on investment, but also about a vast range of societal considerations, from political optimization to need considerations, equity and justice.

NDPC, over the years has prioritized policies taking into consideration the Government's flagship projects, sector priorities and on-going initiatives as well as varied interests of other stakeholders. Using the economic, social and environmental costs and benefits analysis however comes an additional ingredient hammering on cost effectiveness in prioritising future policies. NDPC will therefore use this compendium to inform our conversations and guide decision-makers in setting priorities for Ghana for the coming years. We particularly believe this value-for-money approach would influence the conversation on the Medium-Term National Development Policy Framework and plans.

In this book, you will find succinct overviews of various individual research analyses across a wide range of opportunities for Ghana. The information, however, has to be applied within policy development ambience to obtain real-world impacts. I am therefore enthused that some of Ghana's most distinguished economists participated in the Eminent panel, and discussed all these academic papers over three days in Accra, aimed at finding the best priorities for Ghana's development. The panel consisted of the Minister for Finance Mr. Ken Ofori-Atta, the Minister for Planning Prof. George Gyan-Baffour, a former Finance Minister Prof. Kwesi Botchwey, Prof. Augustin Fosu from the University of Ghana, Prof. Ernest Aryeetey, Secretary-General of the African Research Universities Alliance, Prof. Eugenia Amporfu, a professor of economics at Kwame Nkrumah University of Science and Technology and the Nobel Laureate economist Prof. Finn Kydland.

You may peruse their joint priorities and their individual comments at the concluding pages of this book. Their rankings of their priority policy areas towards the development of Ghana are key pointers. Digital revenue collection was ranked the topmost among the lot. This is obviously a significant priority for a digital Ghana, as President Nana Addo Dankwa Akufo-Addo has repeatedly pointed out and it is one of the identified key flagship interventions for the second term. This digitalisation of revenue collection would focus in Ghana's municipalities through the implementation of a software- District Local Revenue (dLRev). The cost to benefit proportion is nine times meaning for each cedi invested we gain 9 cedis. Digitalisation would ensure a faster data collection process, improved efficiency and increased revenue for the municipalities. This they can used to provide better services to their constituents. As the Finance Ministry pointed out in the justifying its ranking: "Nothing happens without revenue availability."

Another very important issue which was placed as number two, is near-universal coverage of testing and treatment for malaria, which will yield phenomenal societal returns of 133 cedis for every cedi spent. By properly diagnosing malaria and giving early treatment to those infected, 435,000 severe cases and close to 25,000 deaths could be avoided between now and 2030.

Improving maternal and child health was ranked third. The panel embraced research that showed the potential of scaling up the Ghana Essential Health Intervention Program (GEHIP) implemented in Northern Ghana. If this was expanded to include 100% of Ghana's rural population, GEHIP would reduce neonatal mortality by 10% on average over 7 years, saving the lives of 7,551 new born children. In the report every cedi spent will generate benefits for society worth 38 cedis.

Another important focus for Ghana is land titling, which is ranked as the fourth. This programme would survey and document over more than half of Ghana's land area - 170,000 square kilometres of customary lands - to build a comprehensive and automated national base land map. The benefits would include increased property value of titled land, improved access to credit, higher certainty for investments and smoother land transactions. Every cedi spent on the reform could yield benefits of around 90 cedis.

Three interventions to deal with the burden of tuberculosis, which causes five percent of all deaths, were included in the panel's top-10: education and counselling alongside directly observed treatment short-course (DOTS) to make sure those receiving TB treatment adhere to the necessary treatment; improved speed and accuracy of diagnosis through implementation of molecular diagnostic tools; and active case finding in high-risk populations. In this analysis, every cedi spent on these interventions will yield impressive social and economic benefits worth 190, 166 and 38 cedis per cedi spent respectively, highlighting the importance and the potentials of addressing TB as a priority.

Other promising strategies from their top 10 include ambulance maintenance in rural areas, preventive malaria medicine for children in Guinea Savannah, and complementary feeding promotion to reduce childhood malnutrition.

The findings of the Eminent Panel, published in this book, are a particularly important contribution because it highlights the thought leaders interpretation of the research into a simple prioritised list to support improved decision-making. The project has produced a wealth of innovative and informative findings, to highlight a focus on potential solutions rather than the problems. The subsequent action and response are even more important. In this regard, this book is the opening of a conversation, rather than the conclusion. The series of dialogues between Ghana Priorities and the various ministries and departments on the impact per cedi spent have great potential to facilitate the application of the research results in ways that will transform communities in a more sustainable manner.

The NDPC will in response increase its use of cost-benefit analysis as one of the methodologies for facilitating effective policies for Ghana and contribute to the prioritization for the national policy development framework. The outcomes of the Ghana Priorities will also be a significant source of information that would complement other sources for guiding and shaping the policy discourse in the country.

It should be noted that there are 31 million Ghanaians and likely 31 million different opinions about the best ways towards prosperity. The Ghana Priorities research offers an objective data-driven approach to compare different proposals and choices. The ranking from the seven eminent economists, and this book will help kick-start the conversation on priorities and the value-for-money choices. I am looking forward for an engaging and a participatory debate in determining the medium-term development priorities of the country.

Kodjo Esseim Mensah-Abrampa (PhD)
Director General,
National Development Planning Commission
Accra, February 20 2021

CONTRIBUTORS

Dr Bjorn Lomborg is president of the Copenhagen Consensus Center and visiting professor at Copenhagen Business School. The Copenhagen Consensus Center is a think-tank that researches the smartest ways to do good. For this work, Lomborg was named one of TIME magazine's 100 most influential people in the world. His numerous books include "The Skeptical Environmentalist", "Cool It", "How to Spend $75 Billion to Make the World a Better Place" and "The Nobel Laureates' Guide to the Smartest Targets for the World 2016-2030." In 2016, Prospect Magazine awarded Copenhagen Consensus Center, US International Affairs Think Tank of the Year.

Professor Samuel Kobina Annim is a Ghanaian Professor of Economics with specific concentration on micro development economics and applied micro econometrics, statistician and the current, Government Statistician, Ghana Statistical Service.

Dr. Ralph E. Nordjo is currently with Copenhagen Consensus Center and the Project Manager of Ghana Priorities. Worked with BUSAC Fund, Improving Business Practice (IBP) and as a consultant to the Skills Development Fund. His research interests include private sector development, development finance and poverty analysis.

PANEL OF EMINENT ECONOMISTS

The Eminent Panel members met and put questions to the researchers at a three-day academic conference in Accra, Ghana, in August 2020. The Eminent Panel consists of:

Mr. Ken Ofori-Atta is a Ghanaian economist and an investment banker and co-founder of Databank in Ghana. He currently serves as Ghana's Minister for Finance. He was appointed by President Nana Akufo-Addo on 10th January 2017. Mr. Ofori-Atta was the first African to be honoured as a Donaldson Fellow at Yale University in 2010, a John Jay Fellow at Columbia University in 2011 and also a Henry Crown Fellow of the Aspen Institute. He is a Co-Founder of the Aspen African Leadership Initiative. He received a BA in Economics from Columbia University in New York and an MBA from the Yale School of Management.

Prof. George Gyan-Baffour is a Ghanaian development economist and politician. He is a member of the New Patriotic Party and the former Minister of Planning in Ghana. He was a professor at Howard University in Washington, D.C., from 1993 to 2001. He has a post-doctoral diploma from Harvard University, and obtained his masters and PhD at University of Wisconsin, Madison. He graduated with a BA in Economics from the University of Ghana, and proceeded to obtain a Diploma in Economics at the Helsinki School of Economics in Finland.

Prof. Sister Euginia Amporfu is an Associate Professor in the Department of Economics at Kwame Nkrumah University of Science and Technology (KNUST). She holds a PhD in Economics from Simon Fraser University, Burnaby, Canada, and she serves as an External Director on the Governing Board of the Bank of Ghana. She is a member of the Fiscal Council Ghana.

Prof. Kwesi Botchwey is currently the Executive Chairman of the African Development Policy Ownership Initiative and Professor of Practice in Development Economics at The Fletcher School of Law and Diplomacy of Tufts University. Prof. Botchwey was Ghana's Minister for Finance from 1982 to 1995. He received his secondary school education at the Presbyterian Boys' Senior High School in Ghana. He holds an LL.B. from the University of Ghana, a LL.M from Yale Law School, and a doctorate from the University of Michigan Law School. He taught at the University of Zambia, the University of Dar es Salaam in Tanzania, and the University of Ghana.

Prof. Augustin Fosu is Professor, Institute of Statistical, Social and Economic Research (ISSER), University of Ghana. He also holds a number of (honorary) appointments, including: Extraordinary Professor, Faculty of Economic and Management Sciences, University of Pretoria, South Africa; BWPI Research Associate, University of Manchester, UK; and CSAE Research Associate, University of Oxford, UK. His previous positions include: Deputy Director, UN University-WIDER, Finland (2006-2013); Senior Policy Advisor/Chief Economist, UN Economic Commission for Africa, Ethiopia (2004- 2006); and Director of Research, African Economic Research Consortium, Kenya (1998-2004). He holds a PhD in economics from Northwestern University, USA. He has published widely, with certain rankings listing him among 'top economists/authors' in Africa and globally. He is a member of the Fiscal Council Ghana.

Professor Ernest Aryeetey is the Secretary-General of the African Research Universities Alliance (ARUA) and a former Vice-Chancellor of the University of Ghana. Prior to his appointment as Vice-Chancellor, he was a Senior Fellow and Director of the Africa Growth Initiative at the Brookings Institution, Washington, D.C. He was also Director of the Institute of Statistical, Social and Economic Research (ISSER) of the University of Ghana, Legon for the period February 2003 – January 2010.

Prof. Finn Erling Kydland is a Norwegian economist known for his contributions to business cycle theory. He is the Henley Professor of Economics at the University of California, Santa Barbara. He also holds the Richard P. Simmons Distinguished Professorship at the Tepper School of Business of Carnegie Mellon University, where he earned his Ph.D., and a part-time position at the Norwegian School of Economics (NHH). Kydland was a co-recipient of the 2004 Nobel Memorial Prize in Economics, with Edward C. Prescott, "for their contributions to dynamic macroeconomics: the time consistency of economic policy and the driving forces behind business cycles."

Academic Researchers

Abena D. Oduro, Associate Professor of Economics, Department Of Economics, University Of Ghana

Ahmed Issahaku, Department of Civil Engineering, KNUST, Kumasi Ghana

Austin Ablo, Professor of Geography, University of Ghana.

Bahman Kashi, Founder & CEO, Limestone Analytics. Adjunct Professor, Department Of Economics, Queen's University

Bismark Dwumfour-Asare, Senior Lecturer, Environmental Sanitation Department of Environmental Health & Sanitation, University of Education Winneba

Bjorn Larsen, Independent Consultant, Economist, Oslo, Norway

Brad Wong, Chief Economist, Copenhagen Consensus Center

Caroline Reindorf Amissah, Mental Health Authority, Accra, Ghana

Charles Ackah, Senior Research Fellow ISSER And CSPS, University of Ghana

Charles Adjasi, Professor of Development Finance & Economics Stellenbosch University, Cape Town, South Africa

Charles Okyere, Lecturer, Department of Agricultural Economics and Agribusiness, University of Ghana

Daniel Chachu, Department of Economics, University of Ghana

Dr. Eric Arthur, Lecturer, Department Of Economics, KNUST

Dr. Jacob Novignon Lecturer, Department Of Economics, KNUST

Edmund Wedam, Kanmiki Health Systems Researcher Regional Institute For Population Studies, University of Ghana

Edward Nketiah-Amponsah, Associate Professor of Economics, University of Ghana

Emmanuel Abbey, African Universities Alliance, Ghana

Emmanuel Ekow, Asmah School of Economics, University of Cape Coast

Esi Awuah, Department of Civil Engineering, KNUST, Kumasi Ghana

Festus Ebo Turkson, Department of Economics, University of Ghana

Festus Ebo Turkson, Department of Economics, University of Ghana

Fetus Ebo Turkson, Senior Lecturer, Department of Economics, University of Ghana

Francis K. Andoh, School of Economics, University of Cape Coast

Francis Kemausuor, Director The Brew-Hammond Energy Centre, KNUST, Kumasi, Ghana

Freda Asem, Lecturer, Department of Agricultural Economics and Agribusiness, University of Ghana

George Domfe, Senior Research Fellow Centre For Social Policy Studies, University of Ghana

Godfred A. Bokpin, Economist and Professor of Finance Department of Finance, University of Ghana Business School, University of Ghana

Haruna Issahaku Department of Economics, University For Development Studies, Ghana

Jamie Rudman, London School of Hygiene & Tropical Medicine

John Bosco Dramani, Lecturer, Department of Economics, Kwame University of Science and Technology, Ghana, Kumasi

Johnson W Appiah Kubi, Lecturer Centre For Migration Studies, University of Ghana

Justice Nonvignon, Department of Health Policy, Planning and Management, School of Public Health, University of Ghana, Legon, Ghana

Justina Onumah Senior Research Scientist, CSIR-Science and Technology Policy Research Institute

Kwadwo Opoku, Research Fellow CSPS, University of Ghana

Kwaku Amaning Adjei, Senior Lecturer and Fellow at The Brew-Hammond Energy Centre, KNUST, Kumasi, Ghana

Martha Osei Marfo, Department of Water and Sanitation UCC, Cape Coast, Ghana

Martin Oteng-Ababio, Professor of Geography, University of Ghana.

Mawuenyega Makafui Butu, Department of Economics, University of Ghana

Maxwell Dalaba, Research Fellow, Navrongo Health Research Centre, Ghana. Institute of Health Research, University of Allied Sciences, Ho, Ghana

Michael Graham, Professor, University of Stellenbosch Business School, South Africa

Micheal Addo Aziatsi, Department of Civil Engineering, KNUST, Kumasi, Ghana

Monica P. Lambon-Quayefio, Lecturer, Department of Economics, University of Ghana

Nkechi S. Owoo, Senior Lecturer, Department of Economics, University of Ghana

Patrick Opoku Asuming, Economist & Senior Lecturer University of Ghana School of Business

Paul Kwame Nkegbe, Dean of Economics, Department of Economics, University For Development Studies, Ghana

Paul T. Gbahabo, Research Assistant, University of Stellenbosch Business School, South Africa

Peter A. Bah-Lano, Municipal Works Engineer GA East Municipal Assembly

Peter Quartey, Institute of Statistical, Social and Economic Research, University of Ghana

Prince Boakye Frimpong Lecturer, Department of Economics, Kwame University of Science and Technology, Kumasi, Ghana

Priscilla Twumasi Baffour, Department of Economics, University of Ghana

Priscilla Twumasi Baffour, Lecturer, Department of Economics, University of Ghana

Prof. Eugenia Amporfu Associate Professor of Economics Department of Economics, KNUST, Kumasi, Ghana

Rein Houben, London School of Hygiene & Tropical Medicine

Richmond Aryeetey, Associate Professor of Public Health Nutrition, School of Public Health, University of Ghana

Robert Darko Osei, Associate Professor Isser, University of Ghana

Saleema Razvi, Researcher, Copenhagen Consensus Center

Sampson Oduro-Kwarteng, Department of Civil Engineering, KNUST, Kumasi, Ghana

Samuel Agyei Agyemang Department of Health Policy, Planning and Management, School of Public Health, University of Ghana, Legon, Ghana

Sarah Carello, Researcher, Limestone Analytics

Sheetal Silal, Senior Lecturer, University of Cape Town

Stanislaus Adiaba Head Delivery and Compliance Unit Lands Commission, Ghana

Timothy Awine, Phd Candidate, University of Cape Town

Wisdom Akpalu Dean, School of Research and Graduate Studies Ghana Institute of Management and Public Administration (GIMPA)

Wisdom Akpalu, Dean, School of Research and Graduate Studies Ghana Institute of Management and Public Administration (GIMPA)

Yaw Adusi Poku, National TB Control Program, Ghana

Yaw Ofori-Appiah, Research Assistant Department of Agricultural Economics and Agribusiness, University of Ghana

Advisory and Implementation Council

Professor Samuel Kobina Annim is a Ghanaian Professor of Economics with specific concentration on micro development economics and applied micro econometrics, statistician and the current, Government Statistician, Ghana Statistical Service.

Professor Peter Quartey is a Professor of Economics at the Institute of Statistical, Social and Economic Research (ISSER) and Head of the Department of Economics at the University of Ghana. His research interests include private sector development, development finance, monetary economics, migration and remittances, and poverty analysis.

Dr. Felix Addo-Yobo is Director of Policy at the National Development Planning Commission. His specialties include project Management, Urban Drainage, Flood Risk Management, Water Supply and Sanitation, Solid Waste Management, Consumer behavior, Green Economy, Climate Change Adaptation and Mitigation.

Dr. Kodjo Mensah Abrampah is currently the Director General of the National Development Planning Commission. He was the Senior Technical Adviser to the Minister for Planning in Ghana and a member of the technical team that developed the Coordinated Program of the President of Ghana (2017-2024) and currently facilitating its dissemination.

Mr. Emmanuel Kofi Ennin is currently a Technical Assistant to the Finance Minister of Ghana, with a primary responsibility for Monitoring, Evaluation and Reporting on budget Implementation as well as Economic relations with Bilateral and Multilateral Development Partners. He is also the liaison Officer between the Minister, Cabinet and the Economic Management Team (EMT). He was previously an Assistant Manager with Standard Chartered Bank, Ghana.

Dr. Ralph E. Nordjo is currently with Copenhagen Consensus Center and the Project Manager of Ghana Priorities. Worked with BUSAC Fund, Improving Business Practice (IBP) and as a consultant to the Skills Development Fund. His research interests include private sector development, development finance and poverty analysis.

Reference Group Members

A team at the Ministry of Finance led by Dr. K M Abrampah, Senior Technical Advisor

A team at the Ministry of Planning led by Eva Mends, Coordinating Director (Technical)

A team at the National Development Planning Commission led by Dr. Felix Addo-Yobo, Deputy Director (Environmental Policy)

Prof Kwesi Botchwey, former Finance Minister and Ghana Priorities Eminent Panel member

Prof Augustin Fosu, ISSER and Ghana Priorities Eminent Panel member

Pe Ditundini Adiali Ayagitam II, Chief Chiana-Pio

Nii Okwei kinka Dowuona VI, Paramount Chief of Osu Tradition

Rt. Rev. Samuel Osabutey, National Peace Council

Nana Osei Bonsu, Private Enterprise Foundation

AM Baba Alhassan, Zongo Development Fund

Jerry Shaib, Coastal Development Authority

Stephen Y-E Engmen, Northern Development Authority

Joe Danquah, Middle Belt Authority

Prof Samuel Annim, Ghana Statistical Services

Prof Peter Quartey, Ghana University

Farmer A. Morrison, Chamber of Agribusiness

C Aheto Tsegah, former DG Ghana Education Service

Kobby Asmah, Daily Graphics

Bernard Avle, CitiFM

Thomas Ewuntomah, Ghana Immigration Services

Kwesi Ofori, Ghana Police

How to Read this Book to Get the Most Out of It

This book is the result of our collaboration with a wide range of economists, experts, and researchers from Ghana and around the world, spanning sectors like education, governance, health, nutrition, infrastructure and so many more, to identify and shift attention to the best policies for Ghana, giving its citizens a better chance at a more prosperous future. Since resources are limited everywhere, we believe economic prioritization should be included in any serious debate about policy planning and decision-making for every country, not just Ghana.

Each of these short chapters was written in the first instance as a newspaper article and published in Ghana's leading newspaper, *The Daily Graphic.* They have now been edited and refined for this book.

There are many ways you could read this book, the most obvious being from cover to cover. But if you're like most people, you probably have only a handful of policy areas that really matter to you. If that's the case, flip to the table of contents, find the policy areas that interest you, and go straight to the relevant chapters.

You don't have to read the chapters in any specific order to get the most out of the book, but we do think each chapter is worth the read. Our argument is simple: from a policy standpoint, challenge areas are usually complex. As a result, solutions in one area usually rely on and affect other areas.

For more information on the Ghana Priorities project, including the content of this book, visit www.ghanapriorities.com

We hope that you enjoy reading this book as much as we enjoyed putting it together.

Thanks for reading!

Introduction

by Bjorn Lomborg

The Ghanaian economy has been growing swiftly, with remarkable GDP growth higher than five per cent for two years running.

This robust growth means added pressure from special interest groups who demand more public spending on certain projects.

But like every country, Ghana lacks the money to do everything that citizens would like. It has to prioritise between many worthy opportunities.

Many campaigners have compelling stories on how these extra resources should be spent best to improve Ghana's wellbeing and prosperity. Some point to research showing that education improves a nation's health and economy for generations. Others argue that there are great potentials to be achieved in healthcare, water and sanitation, infrastructure, or fisheries.

But even within these broad areas, what should decision-makers prioritise? Within education, should extra resources be focussed on improving foundational skills or encourage vocational training and apprenticeships? Should the first health focus be tuberculosis or hypertension? Should we focus our efforts to improve sanitation in urban or rural areas?

There are as many opinions as there are Ghanaians. But the biggest problem with setting spending priorities is that there is little information on the cost of such interventions and even less on the benefits.

Most pundits base their answers on own experience and emotions, or on their knowledge of one sector or another. These are powerful and important. But they cannot replace data as a firm and fair foundation for important decision-making. Even strategic plans from the government or donors encounter this problem: there is a lack of comprehensive information about Ghana's challenges and the best solutions.

What if economic science and data could help cut through the noise from interest groups, and guide the allocation of additional money, to improve the budgeting process and ensure that each cedi can do even more for Ghana?

Cost-benefit analysis – an approach that uses rigorous, cross-sector analysis to establish what could be achieved by spending additional money in different areas – is rarely used by any government in the world in a broad, transparent fashion.

Why? Because it requires large numbers of academics, well-organised inputs and the collection of considerable data, and because it creates analytical results that can upset some vested interest groups.

I head the award-winning think tank, Copenhagen Consensus Center and we have been fortunate to work together with the National Development Planning Commission, the NDPC to create the Ghana Priorities, whose outcome you are reading just now.

What can such a project realistically achieve for Ghana? The country has huge opportunities ahead – but also challenges which could impact prosperity if not navigated carefully.

Ghana is undertaking great efforts to diversify its economy, but like in many nations, the economy can still be buffeted by changes in commodity prices. Which investments and settings could best help businesses to thrive?

Like other middle-income countries, chronic non-communicable diseases have overtaken infectious diseases as the biggest health care burden.

At the same time, reducing malaria and maternal mortality still remain public health concerns, and rural-urban disparities on vital issues such as infrastructure or access to education and health care need to be overcome to ensure all Ghanaians benefit from the positive economic development.

What investments will make sure these challenges are addressed in the most efficient manner?

Whether we look at these challenges, or at how to improve public services, how to reduce plastic pollution in Accra, the swiftest way to continue Ghana's reduction in poverty, or the best approach to expand education and social assistance programmes to all, cost-benefit analysis can help focus attention on the investments that would have the biggest impact.

The NDPC and Copenhagen Consensus have been fortunate to work with a wide range of eminent experts and economist throughout Ghana, from its universities, ministries, sectors and NGOs. They have highlighted not just smart policies within specific areas but shown us *how much* policies will cost and *how much* good it will end up doing.

Of course, not all proposals are politically palatable and attract public interest – but many will, and those smart programmes can help budgets go even further.

Showing where each cedi does the most good does not offer the last word in budgetary decision-making or supplant politicians; it merely ensures that citizens and politicians are better informed.

In Ghana's 2019 budget, spending increased by 27 per cent or GH₵15.6bn.

Imagine if just two per cent of this increase would be spent even more effectively because of the Ghana Priorities research.

That would, over the next decade generate social benefits larger than the entire Ghanaian GDP last year.

That is a conversation worth having.

OVERVIEW OF THE SOCIAL, ECONOMIC AND ENVIRONMENTAL VALUE PER CEDI SPENT

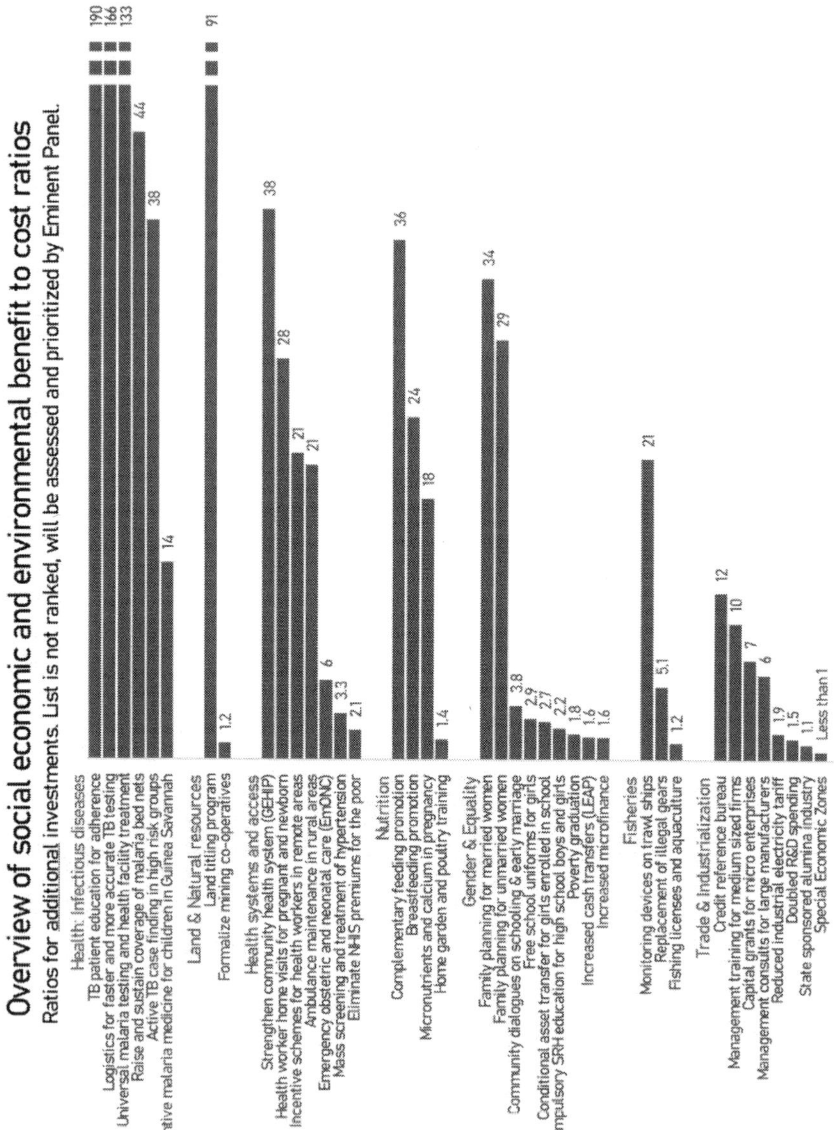

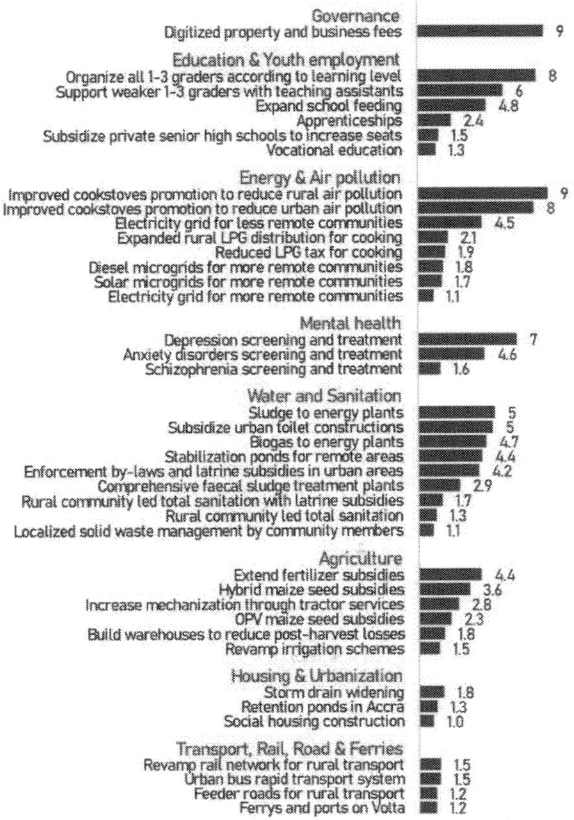

GHANA PRIORITIES

All benefit-cost ratios are comparable. If you spend on promoting improved cookstoves, the social, economic, and environmental benefits are 9 times the cost. Each cedi spent on extending fertilizer subsidies for smallholder farmers will do 4.4 cedis of social and economic good. In principle, all benefits are included. The benefits of providing family planning is not only avoided child and maternal deaths, but also increased economic growth from the demographic dividend. Summaries and academic papers behind these numbers are available on www.ghanapriorities.com

Transforming Ghana's agricultural sector

Agriculture is a significant contributor to the Ghanaian economy and an important source of employment, with over 40% of all workers engaged in farming. With growth and development, the country is gradually shifting away from this sector towards industry and services, but agriculture is still key for the economy, and a necessary vehicle for reducing poverty and food insecurity.

Increasing agricultural output is an important policy goal of the government, and can be achieved through three main mechanisms: increasing area under cultivation, improving the yield, and reducing post-harvest losses, all areas in which there's currently room for improvement.

Only about 64% of the total agriculture land area of Ghana is cultivated, 30% of agricultural land is under mechanization and the use of improved seeds and fertilizer is low. Post-harvest losses are also relevant, reaching about 18% of the country's annual maize production.

To improve the agricultural sector's production efficiency and post-harvest management, a group of researchers, namely Robert Darko Osei, Freda Asem, Charles Yaw Okyere, Wilson Appiah-Kubi, Justina Onumah and Yaw Ofori-Appiah from the University of Ghana and Brad Wong of Copenhagen Consensus analysed the cost and benefits of improved seeds and fertilizer, irrigation and mechanization to increase yields, and warehouses to reduce post-harvest losses.

Improved seeds can increase agricultural yields, but their use is still low in Ghana, mostly due to their high cost and lack of information among smallholder farmers. Subsidies for improved seeds for maize production could boost their usage by 30% and have a substantial effect on yield.

The researchers estimated the total cost of this intervention at GH₵ 490 million for the highly efficient hybrid seeds and GH₵

510 million for the popular open-pollinated variety (OPV), but the benefit in higher agricultural yields would be worth nearly GHC 1.8 billion with hybrid seeds and close to GHC 1.2 billion with OPV. Every cedi spent on this intervention would bring a return 2.3 to 3.6 times higher than the original investment.

Fertilizer use is also below the optimal levels among smallholder farmers, so the researchers examined the economic viability of maintaining the current 50% subsidy so that farmers can afford the required quantities. After 5 years the subsidies would gradually be lowered as farmers would benefit from higher yields. In total, the costs amount to GHC 460 million, but the intervention would increase fertilizer use by 27% and result in a benefit of GHC 2 billion, over 4 times higher than the cost.

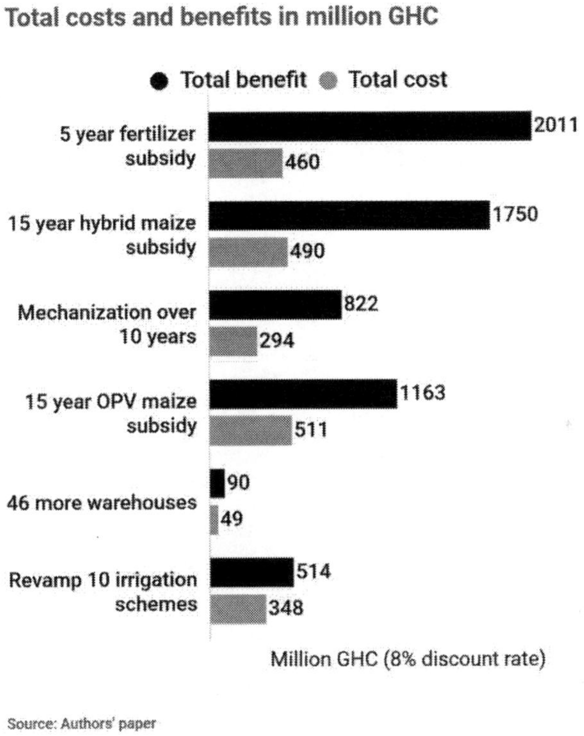

The scarcity of water is an additional limiting factor for crops and climate change aggravates the situation, so the economists studied the possibility of rehabilitating 10 existing irrigation sites to cover a total area of 3,400 hectares. While the government would cover the cost of rehabilitation, the cost of ongoing maintenance would be borne by farmers in the form of user fees. Implementing this programme was estimated to cost GH₵ 360 million over three years, but it would result in benefits worth over GH₵ 510m over a 10-year period, 1.5 times the cost of the original investment.

Mechanization is essential for improving agricultural productivity but remains low among Ghana's smallholder farmers. An intervention to increase the area under mechanization by 13% in 10 years through purchasing additional tractors and implements to improve soil quality and higher plant growth would cost nearly GH₵ 300 million. However, the benefit would be an 11% increase in yields and overall agricultural output.

This benefit would amount to over GH₵ 820 million by 2039, which means every cedi spent on this initiative would generate nearly three cedis in benefit.

Investing in post-harvest loss reduction is another pathway for stabilizing prices, ensuring food security and reducing poverty. The researchers looked at constructing 46 new warehouses with an average capacity of 1,000 tonnes to curb post-harvest storage losses. For the entire 15 years of this intervention, the costs are estimated at GH₵ 50 million, but the benefits in post-harvest losses avoided, stability and an eventual reduction of prices amount to GH₵ 90 million, nearly double the cost.

Ghana's agricultural sector has great potential for improvement through smart investments in the right policies and modernized technologies. Altogether, these five interventions provide policymakers interesting new inputs to help improve food security, reduce poverty and increase agricultural exports to boost the country's economy.

Interventions	BCR	Benefit (GHȻ Million)	Cost (GHȻ Million)
Fertilizer subsidy (27% usage increase for 5 years, reduced to 5% increase during 5 years phase-out)	4.4	2,011	460
Improved seeds subsidy (11% annual usage growth over 15 years)			
Hybrid Maize	3.6	1,750	490
OPV Maize	2.3	1,163	511
Increase area under mechanization with 13% over 10 years	2.8	822	294
Increase maize warehouse capacity by 46,000 tonnes	1.8	90	49
Revamping 10 irrigation schemes covering 3,443 ha	1.5	514	348

Total costs and benefits are discounted at 8%

Interventions for smallholder farmers

Social value for money (benefit-cost ratio)

1. **4.4x Fertilizer**
   Maintained 50% price subsidy increasing the usage by 27% for 5 years, then phase-out over 5 years to 26% price subsidy

2. **3.6x Hybird maize seeds**
   Price subsidy for improved seeds by 50% resulting in 11% annual usage growth over 15 years

3. **2.8x Mechanization**
   Increase area under mechanization with 13% over 10 years

4. **2.3x OPV maize seeds**
   Price subsidy for improved OPV seeds by 50% resulting in 11% annual usage growth over 15 years

5. **1.8x Warehouse capacity**
   Increase maize warehouses capacity by 46,000 tonnes by building and operating 46 new warehouses

6. **1.5x Irrigation schemes**
   Revamping 10 existing irrigation schemes covering 3,443 ha

Source: Authors' computations using 8% discount rate

THE BEST ACTIONS TO EMPOWER GIRLS AND REDUCE POVERTY

About Fifty-one percent. This is the alarming dropout rate of Ghanaian girls who do not complete junior high school. Many drop out to get married. Child marriage is a common practice that affects 4 out of every 10 girls in sub-Saharan Africa. In Ghana, 27% of girls are married before reaching the legal age.

Source: 2014 Ghana Demographic and Health Survey report

The percentage is even higher in rural areas and among the poorest population, particularly in the Northern Regions, where it has increased in recent years, impelled by cultural practices and poverty. Parents are forced to marry off their daughters to strengthen relationships between families or to gain wealth in the form of livestock. While laws exist to prevent this situation, their enforcement has had limited effects.

Child marriage has a physical, intellectual, psychological and emotional impact, from teenage pregnancies and their complications to keeping girls from finishing school. It has been identified as a potential driver that sustains poverty and affects the entire society, which makes child marriage an important issue for policymakers to address.

To study the impact of child marriage, Abena Oduro and George Domfe from the University of Ghana and Brad Wong from the Copenhagen Consensus focused on three interventions aimed at the economic, structural and social factors behind it. They studied a community dialogues project, a conditional asset transfer to the families, and educational support, to determine the smartest ways to focus government spending on this issue.

These three interventions were each tested in Burkina Faso, Ethiopia, and Tanzania, with promising results.

The community dialogues intervention aims to educate and sensitize on the negative impacts of child marriage. In most cases girls do not have a say in the decision, which is why the intervention targets their families and communities in weekly focus groups, offering them a space to contribute and gain insights.

The cost of this intervention, including training and organization of the dialogues, was calculated at less than GH₵ 9 million, for the communities of 63,000 girls. The researchers estimate this will avoid more than 6,000 early marriages and prevent many health conditions caused by intimate partner violence and adolescent pregnancy, including maternal and infant deaths. They calculated the total benefits at GH₵ 33 million, which means every cedi spent would generate social good worth almost 4 cedi.

Conditional asset transfers tackle the economic problem at the root of child marriage by reducing the economic pressure on the family, providing the household an additional income source. This intervention comprises the transfer of an asset, typically livestock, to the parents, if the girls remain unmarried and successfully complete the academic year.

The total cost of the asset for about 58,000 girls for the three years of junior high school, including the tuition costs, was calculated at GH₵ 40 million. The benefits, however, are more than 6,800 avoided early marriages and their associated health conditions, and an increase in lifetime earnings for the girls who remain in school. The total benefit of GH₵ 107 million in social and economic good means a return almost three times higher than the original investment.

Finally, the researchers looked at education support to complement Ghana's free basic education policy. Although Ghana provides a free uniform for every child when they start school, most children will require two or more uniforms during their education.

An additional free uniform for girls at the start of each academic year would reduce the cost to parents and increase the probability of the girls staying in school. The cost of the uniforms and schooling for 64,000 junior high school girls was valued at slightly below GH₵ 20 million. The total benefit of this initiative, in turn, was estimated at GH₵ 56 million, which means every cedi spent on this initiative would bring a return of 3 cedis.

Overall, this study suggests that organising community dialogues is the most cost-effective policy option in the fight against child marriage. Reducing the economic pressure on the household is also a good intervention, while education support makes a considerable impact on girls' school retention. All three initiatives would provide households the cultural and economic support needed to help empower girls and reduce poverty.

Interventions	BCR	Benefit (GH₵ Million)	Cost (GH₵ Million)
Dialogues in the communities of 63,000 JHS girls	3.8	32.8	8.6
Free uniforms for 64,000 JHS girls	2.9	56.4	19.5
Asset transfer to parents of 58,000 JHS girls	2.7	107	40.1

Total costs and benefits are discounted at 8%

Keep girls in school to reduce child marriages

Value for money (Cedi social benefits per Cedi spent)

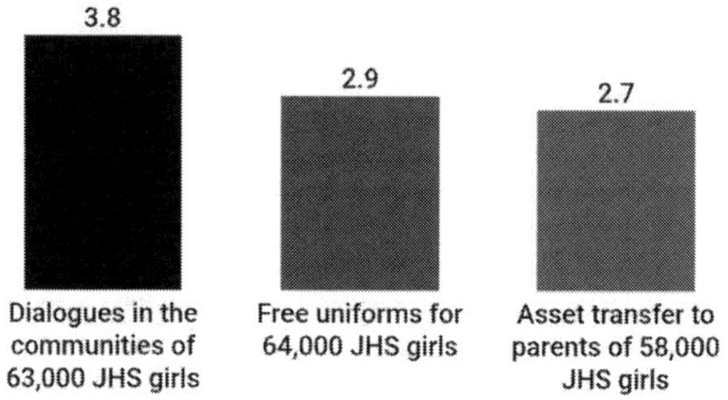

Total cost over 3 years of Junior High School

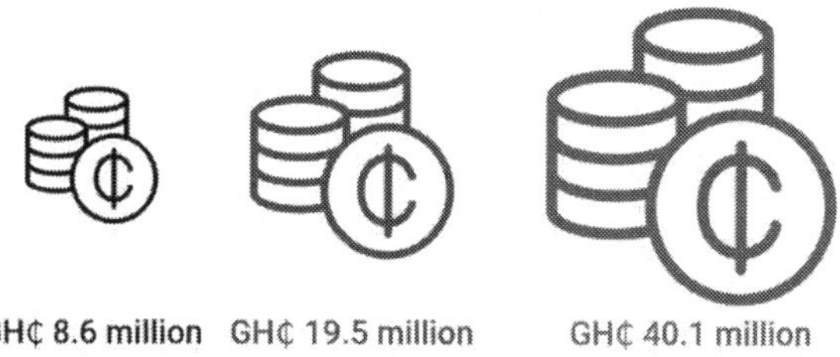

Number of avoided child marriages

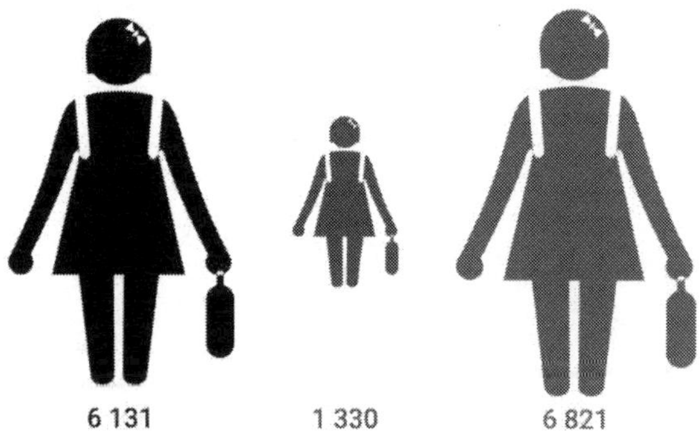

MODERNISED ADMINISTRATION FOR INCREASED AUTONOMY

Digitizing public administration at the local level improves efficiency and productivity. Faster and simpler revenue collection, especially, boosts transparency and increases municipalities' autonomy by enhancing their ability to generate more local income in a systematic manner.

Ghana has a legal decentralization framework that allows for the fiscal autonomy of the Metropolitan, Municipal and District Assemblies (MMDAs) with important planning and coordination functions. The MMDAs are responsible for infrastructure and service delivery in key sectors of public life: waste management, transport, roads, housing, disaster prevention, births and deaths, among others.

However, Ghana's MMDAs still depend on central government transfers to fund their development, generating only approximately 20% of their total budget with their own resources. Streamlined, fast revenue collection has the potential to improve their autonomy, but decision-makers need to ensure they invest limited public resources in the smartest way possible. That's why Ghana Priorities set out to study the effects of digitizing public administration.

To study the digitisation of revenue collection in Ghana's municipalities, researchers for Ghana Priorities have analysed the implementation of a software called District Local Revenue (dLRev) to manage property rate collection.

dLRev is an open-source, web-based data tracking and revenue collection software. It is currently set up for property rates and business operating permits, but can also be used for other revenue items, including rents for district infrastructure, fees and fines, and investment. It is jointly developed and implemented by Ghana's Ministry for Local Government and Rural Development (MLGRD) and the Governance for Inclusive Development

(GovID) programme of the Deutsche Gesellschaft für Internationale Zusammenarbeit (GIZ).

Preconditions for the functioning of the software, e.g. standards for naming streets and assigning property addresses, were jointly created by the project partners over almost a decade.

With a digital address map of a district, a spatial database and a fiscal cadastre of revenue items, dLRev is used to manage data, billing, and collection, and it has already been tested in nine municipalities that have been using the software throughout the year 2019.

For the Ghana Priorities project, the researchers studied the cost and revenue data obtained from these nine municipalities to reach the average costs and benefits over a period of four years.

There are prerequisites anchored on Ghana's legal and policy frameworks for spatial planning and local revenue mobilisation that municipalities need to satisfy in order to use the dLRev software, including developing spatial databases by implementing street-naming and property addressing and establishing fiscal cadastre from property valuation data.

The researchers estimated the total cost for all the different components, including data collection, hardware costs and the training of collectors, at GH₵ 489,000 for an average MMDA over the initial four years of implementation.

The benefits of dLRev are a faster data collection process, improved efficiency and increased revenue for the municipalities. Before, the identification of business and property ratepayers was manual, lasting approximately 120 man-days per 10,000 parcels. With dLRev, the data collectors undergo training and use tablets to upload new information immediately to the address map, which reduces the time of data collection to 20 man-days per 10,000 parcels.

Prior to the introduction of dLRev, most assemblies also issued demand notices to clients for the payment of the rates, rents and other bills, but most of them were hand-written. Even the distribution of bills posed a major challenge for the revenue collectors, as most buildings were not numbered. Therefore prior to dLRev, printing and distribution of bills in the sample municipalities ranged from 15 to as many as 80 days, with an average of 25 days. With the software, this time decreased to only 2 days for the average municipality.

As a result, both the number of ratepayers and the compliance rate increased, and the revenue collected grew by an average of 54% in the first year of implementation. The total benefits of the implementation calculated for an average MMDA are GH₵ 4.3 million, which means each cedi spent on this intervention yields a return nearly nine times higher.

Introducing dLRev is not only cost-effective but a critical tool for better revenue management. The efficient taxation of properties has significant untapped potential for increasing local governments' revenue collection and improving their autonomy. Modernising public administration locally can improve revenue mobilisation substantially, boost efficiency and decentralisation, and give municipalities the tools they need to deliver better services for all Ghanaians.

Interventions	BCR	Benefit (GH₵ Million)	Cost (GH₵ Million)
Digitised property and business fees using dLRev per MMA over 4 years	9	4,300,000	489,000

Total costs and benefits are discounted at 8%

Digitised property rates and business fees

Total costs 488,600 GHC per MMDA over 4 years

Data collection and set-up

Data collection teams usually include National Service personnel, NABCO, and salaried district assembly staff. Necessary data include **aerial imagery for spatial databases, street-naming** and property addressing, property valuation, and fee-fixing.

Training of management

This team comprises a Management Information System (MIS) Officer, Physical Planning Officer (PPO), Finance Officer, Budget Analyst and Coordinating Director.

Hardware & software costs

10-20 tablets for 600 GHS each are enough for a small team. In addition internet bundles for smartphone / tablet. All necessary software are free of charge.

Revenue collector training

The technical team visits the MMDA to provide user training to the dLRev-team for two or three days. The **revenue collectors receive specific training on the distribution** of demand notices.

Notices printing costs

With printing and distribution of demand notices, MMDA needs to change their practices. Regional advisors support MMDAs through this change management process.

Benefits from digitised revenue collection per MMDA

GHC 1.6 million increase in revenues per year

The increased revenue is derived from an increase in the number of ratepayers and an increase in the rate of compliance

Identification of ratepayers

This annual activity usually lasts 120 man-days per 10,000 parcels. Providing a mobile app, the dLRev management software has reduced this to 20 man-days per 10,000 parcels.

Issuing demand notices

Revenue collector man-days to distribute the bills decreased from 25 days to 2 days.

Paying collectors

The time to prepare the paperwork to pay revenue collectors decreased from 20-80 days to 10-20 days.

Further benefits

Widening of the tax base. Automatizing the transaction management process will further reduce potential leakages.

Source: Authors' paper

Improved Learning and Equality

Ghana has made great strides to improve its education system in the past decades, with near-universal primary school enrolment and equal access to schooling between boys and girls. However, as in many other developing countries, the quality of education is still a critical challenge. In a 2016 assessment, 45% and 30% of 4th graders could not meet minimum standards in mathematics and English.

Better-quality learning in schools can increase equality and have a major effect on the country's overall development, but decision-makers need quality evidence for discussions on how to spend the limited resources at their disposal.

That's why Festus Ebo Turkson and Priscilla Twumasi Baffour from the University of Ghana and Brad Wong of Copenhagen Consensus studied two interventions designed to improve learning levels in Ghanaian schools: an expansion of Ghana's School Feeding Program (GSFP), and a pedagogical approach called 'Teaching at the Right Level'.

GSFP was first implemented in 10 schools in 2005 but has since then expanded significantly and today provides one hot meal to 2.8 million children, or 61% of students in public basic school. Children in communities with school feeding have experienced improvements in learning levels and test scores, as well as increased height and weight.

The researchers studied an expansion of the program to 70% of students, approximately 383,000 more children. This expansion would have a total cost of GH₵ 110 million per year, including the cost of food, preparation and logistics, and increased time at school for students and teachers. They found that the intervention wouldn't have a high impact on overall school enrolment, thanks to Ghana's already near-universal levels of enrolment.

However, it would increase learning, especially for two vulnerable sub-groups: children from households below the poverty line and girls. Improved nutrition would lead to increased lifetime productivity and wages and an improvement in nutritional status and health beyond learning impacts.

Overall, the intervention could increase incomes among the beneficiary population by roughly GH₵ 2,300 per student over their lifetimes. The total benefits of this intervention equal GH₵ 526 million per year, nearly five times the original investment.

'Teaching at the Right Level' (TaRL) targets instruction to the specific learning needs of children by splitting them into class groups based on learning levels rather than age, for one or two hours per day. Two forms of TaRL were assessed in this study, one involving all students in grades 1-3 and another focused only on weaker students.

The first option could be delivered by public school teachers to 50% of students in grades 1-3 for a total social cost of GH₵ 87 million per year, consisting mainly of training for teachers, materials and monitoring. As a result, the intervention would provide a modest learning boost to all students worth 1.5% of earnings over their lives, or roughly GH₵ 1040.

The total social benefits of TaRL for all students are over GH₵ 700 million per year, and every cedi spent on this intervention would generate social benefits worth eight cedis.

Another option is to perform the same intervention with a greater focus on weaker students, using teaching community assistants to assist regular teachers. This would be costlier per student — at the same price, it would reach 520,000 students in grades 1-3, nearly covering all of those who did not meet minimum learning standards.

However, the intervention would provide a larger learning improvement for weaker students and increase their earnings by 2.6% over their lifetime, worth GH₵ 1,775. In total, this intervention would generate social benefits worth GH₵ 520 million each year, six times more than the original investment.

Out of these interventions, broad-based TaRL provides the largest benefits to society, but the alternative targeted at weaker students results in higher average gains and could help reduce wage inequality in the future. With school feeding, in turn, a disproportionate share of the benefits are experienced by girls and children from poor households.

Adopting this intervention would make Ghanaian society lose out on GH₵ 200 million of potential benefits per year, but policymakers may deem the equity gains for vulnerable populations to be worth it.

Interventions	BCR	Benefit (GH₵ Million)	Cost (GH₵ Million)
Teaching at the right level for 1.2 million students	8.3	717	87
Teaching at the right level for 520,000 students with lower learning levels	6.0	518	87
Expansion of school feeding to 383,000 students	4.8	526	110

Total costs and benefits are discounted at 8%

Improved learning in primary school

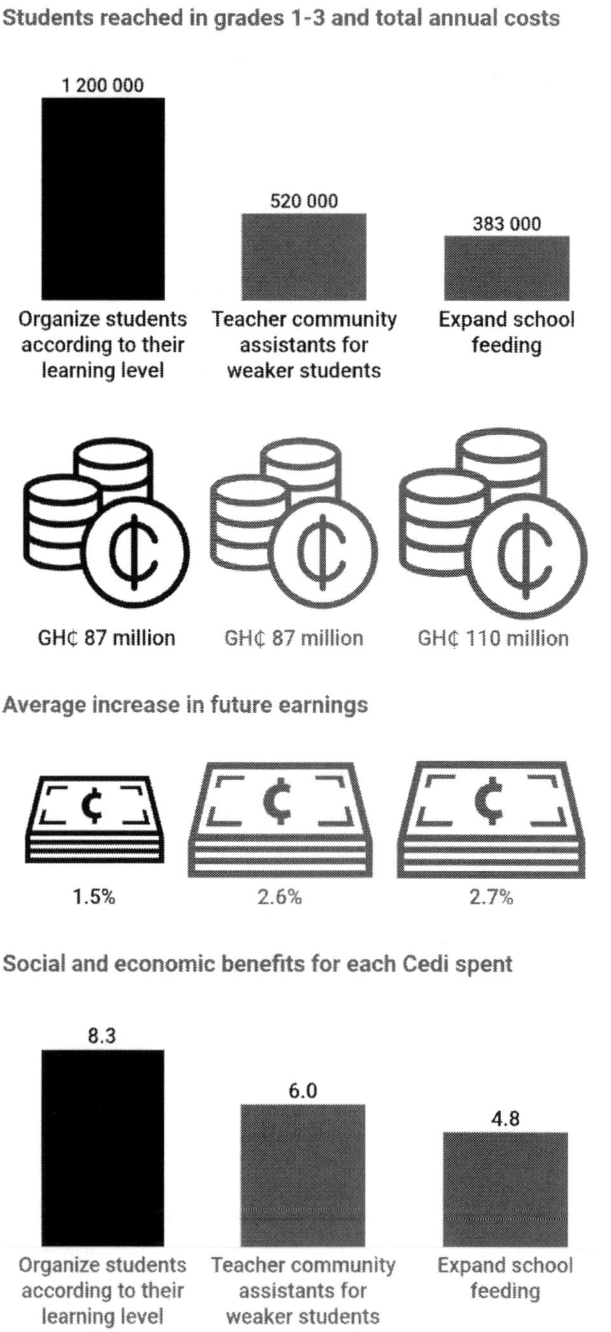

Source: Authors paper assuming 8% discount rate

Family Planning for Health and Development

Family planning plays an important role in the reproductive health and rights of women. Access to contraception helps empower women and adolescents, increases investment in children, and contributes to poverty reduction and overall development. A reduction of 0.5 in the fertility rate has been shown to lead to a 5.6 percent increase in GDP per capita over 20 years. A decrease in unplanned pregnancies also leads to a lower risk of health complications, maternal and child deaths and malnutrition in children.

Securing access to family planning is a critical component of building human capital in most developing countries, but policy-makers need to make sure every cedi spent of limited public resources generates the largest possible benefit in economic and social terms.

To inform the debate on how to improve reproductive health, Prof. Eugenia Amporfu, Dr. Eric Arthur and Dr. Jacob Novignon from the Kwame Nkrumah University of Science and Technology and Dr. Brad Wong of Copenhagen Consensus studied two key interventions: extending Ghana's current family planning programme for adult women and including compulsory sexual health education for boys and girls at the junior high school (JHS) and senior high school (SHS) levels.

Since 2015, Ghana has had a successful family planning programme that has helped increase the use of contraceptives from 32% to 38% among unmarried women and from 22% to 30% with married women. The researchers studied an extension of this policy, increasing the targets for contraception prevalence to 50% and 40% for these two groups of beneficiaries, respectively. This would result in a total of nearly 72,000 unintended pregnancies avoided every year for unmarried women and 81,000 unintended pregnancies avoided for married women. In the long run, this would mean 138 neonatal deaths and 74 maternal deaths averted for unmarried women and 235 neonatal deaths and 126 maternal deaths for married women. The lowered fertility rate would also have an important impact on the economy, through a proportional increase of around 3% of GDP per capita over 20 years.

The total cost of the intervention is GHC 1,012 million for an intervention targeting 3.2 million unmarried women over 8 years and GHC 988 million for an intervention targeting 4.2 million married women over 6 years. The benefits are GHC 30,000 million and GHC 33,000 million, respectively.

Benefits and costs of increased contraception prevalence

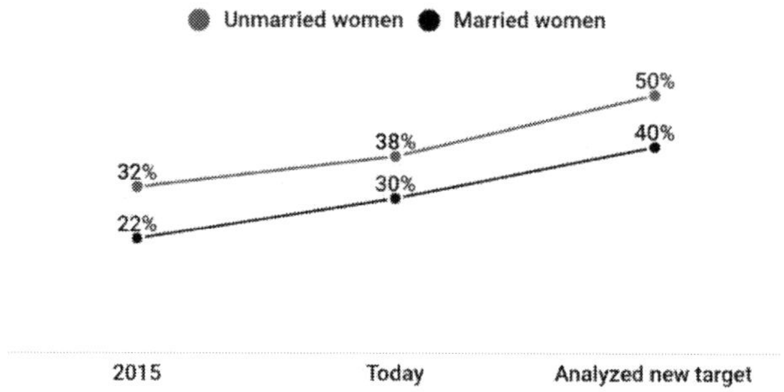

200 maternal lives saved
planned pregnancies leads to a lower risk of health complications

373 neonatal lives saved
avoided child deaths and malnutrition in children

additional benefits
helps empower women and increases investment in children

3% extra per person GDP
reduced fertility rate leads to increased GDP per capita over 20 years

value of benefits 29-34 times the cost
Total estimated cost to achieve the target in 6 to 8 years is GHC 2 billion, total value of benefits is GHC 63 billion

Source: Authors paper assuming 8% discount rate

Targeting married women brings the number of births down by a larger amount, which leads to a higher demographic dividend and therefore an even higher return on investment. Every cedi spent would produce social and economic good worth 29 to nearly 34 cedis.

Teen mothers and their children are at a higher risk of health complications, and less likely to continue with their education. In Ghana, the teenage childbearing rate is 75 births per 1,000 girls, higher than the global average of 44 births. Nearly all sexually active, adolescent and unmarried females want to avoid pregnancy within the next two years, but 62% have an unmet need for family planning and the number of unintended pregnancies during JHS is estimated to be over 56,000.

For this reason, the researchers also analysed an intervention on compulsory, comprehensive, and universal reproductive health education.

Sexual and reproductive health education already forms part of the curriculum in Ghana, but it is not compulsory and the coverage of topics is minimal. Drop-out rates are also considerable. The intervention proposed in the study includes a revision of the curriculum, training of school-based health coordinators, and education on birth control methods such as contraceptives and abstention for one cohort of adolescents through JHS and SHS.

The intervention would avoid over 10,000 unintended pregnancies at JHS level and nearly 4,500 at SHS level.

An effective compulsory, comprehensive sexual education would delay pregnancy to an age when it is physically safer to have children, which reduces the medical costs of birth, fistula, caesareans and abortions, and infant and maternal mortality. Approximately 9 maternal deaths and 118 infant deaths would be averted per cohort thanks to the intervention. Continued education would also provide increased income worth GH₵ 670 per year of JHS and GH₵ 900 per year of SHS completed, lasting for the women's entire working lives.

Benefits and costs of compulsory sexual and reproductive health education for boys and girls in JHS and SHS

Reduction in school drop-out
leads to income boost from education throughout the work life
GHC 670 per year of JHS and GHC 900 per year of SHS completed

Delayed pregnancies
reduce the medical costs of birth, fistula, caesareans and abortions

9 adolescent maternal lives saved
for each cohort of girls and boys throughout JHS and SHS

118 infant lives saved
for each cohort of girls and boys throughout JHS and SHS

cost estimate 127 million cedi
Including improved curriculum, retraining, commodities, additional schooling costs due to fewer dropouts, and administration

value of benefits 2.2 times the cost
Total estimated cost per cohort GHC 127 million,

Source: Authors paper assuming 8% discount rate

The total costs of this intervention were estimated at approximately GHȻ 127 million over a 7-year period and the benefits at GHȻ 285 million, meaning the intervention would provide a benefit around 2 times higher than the original investment.

In both cases, the health and economic benefits exceed the costs of the proposed initiatives. High fertility rates hamper economic growth and development, and intensive interventions that respond to women's contraceptive needs would be a key element in reversing the high rate of unwanted pregnancies in Ghana.

Interventions	BCR	Benefit (GH₵ Million)	Cost (GH₵ Million)
Family planning for 10 percent points more married women	34	33,204	988
Family planning for 12 percent points more unmarried women	29	29,717	1013
Sexual and reproductive health education per cohort through JHS and SHS	2.2	286	127

Total costs and benefits are discounted at 8%

A SUSTAINABLE FUTURE FOR GHANA'S FISHING SECTOR

Fishing makes a substantial contribution to Ghana's economy and employment, sustaining the livelihoods of at least 3 million people, including half a million women. In West Africa, fish constitutes about one-third of animal protein consumed. However, the marine fish stock in Ghana is biologically over-exploited and at risk of collapsing.

Catches have declined in recent decades, small-sized fish have become prevalent, and only 40% of the fish consumed in Ghana today is produced locally. Excess fishing is worsened by illegal, unreported activities and destructive techniques.

Catch per canoe declines while their number increases

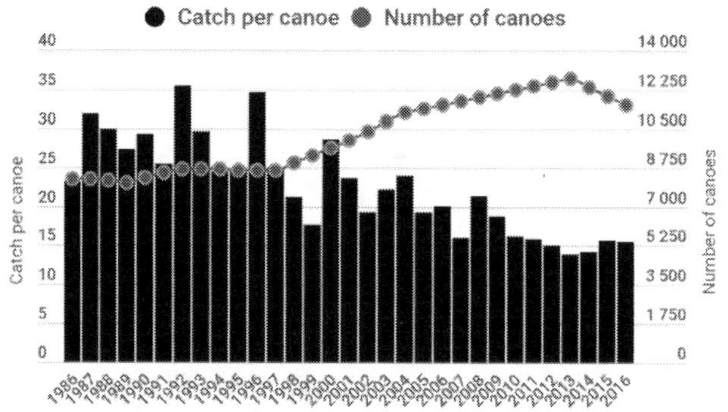

Source: Author's paper

Ghana's fishing sector requires urgent solutions in order to avoid ecological collapse and guarantee a sustainable income to the artisanal fishers and the entire value chain dependent on the activity. The government needs to make sure it is implementing the correct policies to secure the livelihoods of people who rely on this sector, which is why it's crucial to know where public resources should be directed first to generate the highest benefit.

To address the overfishing problem, Prof. Wisdom Akpalu from the University of Ghana analysed three policy interventions: replacing illegal fishing nets, limiting the number of boats while providing training and subsidies for fish farming, and installing video devices in trawl vessels to monitor harmful illegal activities.

Artisanal marine fishery is the livelihood of many coastal communities and the most important sector of fishing in Ghana for GDP, employment, and supply of animal protein. However, approximately nine of every ten artisanal fishermen in Ghana use nets with illegally small mesh sizes, contributing to the depletion of resources by not allowing smaller fishes to grow.

One way to improve this situation is by replacing the illegal nets with legal ones, which will reduce harvest in the short term.

Since the stocks are fast-growing species, within a year, the fish caught will be bigger and more valuable. The intervention would have a total cost of GH₵ 250 million in both the nets and initial loss of income for the fishermen, but in the long run would increase revenue from selling mature fish, more than twice the price of juveniles.

This benefit was calculated to be worth GH₵ 1.3 billion over a 10-year period, approximately 5 times larger than the total cost of the intervention.

To reduce excess fishing in the artisanal sector, the number of canoes should also be reduced. Doing so would increase profits for the remaining boats by GH₵ 107 million per year but lead to 40,000 jobs and GH₵ 66 million of annual income lost. The fishermen who would lose their jobs could be incentivized to take up fish farming in ponds and cages by supporting them through interest-free loans and subsidies for fish feed for four years, until the farming becomes profitable.

This intervention would cost GH₵ 3.8 billion but create revenue worth GH₵ 4.5 billion for both the fish farmers and the remaining fishers, thanks to stock build-up and increased profits. Every cedi spent would return 1.2 cedi, including the added long-term benefit of protecting the marine fishing sector.

The final intervention studied focused on the industrial trawling vessels that operate farther away from the coast. This sector contributes heavily to the overfishing problem both because of the large number of vessels and due to *saiko*, the practice of illegally targeting small, juvenile stocks that could become bigger and more valuable, freezing them into pellets, and shipping them to middlemen for processing, resulting in a poor-quality product.

The intervention aims to install video equipment on each vessel to impede these illegal practices, at an estimated total cost of GH₵ 83 million.

However, the potential increase in profit for artisanal fishers thanks to better stock and a product of better quality would be approximately GH₵ 1.75 billion for the ten-year time period. This intervention would thus bring a benefit 21 times higher than the original investment, if the cameras contributed to better enforcement.

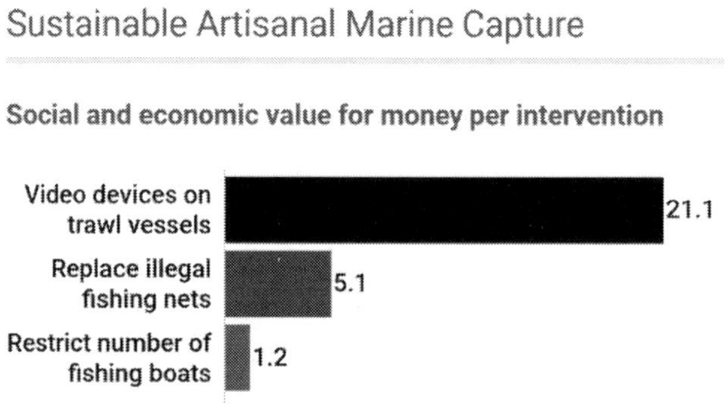

The impact of the activities of trawl vessels on artisanal stocks has serious implications for food security and sustainable livelihoods within and beyond the fishing communities, and halting their illegal catch of small species can generate high benefits.

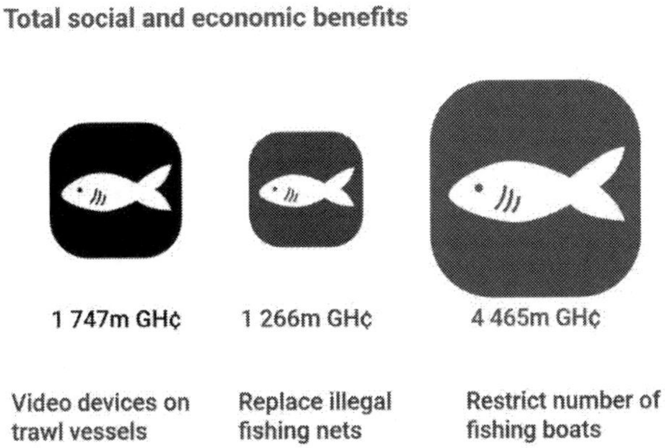

Altogether, these initiatives provide cost-effective measures for policymakers to prevent the collapse of Ghana's marine fish stocks and guarantee a sustainable future for this important sector of the economy.

Interventions	BCR	Benefit (GH₵ Million)	Cost (GH₵ Million)
Planting of video devices on trawl vessels	21.1	1,747	83
Replacement of illegal fishing nets	5.1	1,266	247
Restricting fishing boats while providing training and subsidising feed for aquaculture	1.2	4,465	3,786

Total costs and benefits are discounted at 8%

Improved Access to Free Senior High School

Achieving universal primary and secondary education is a central target of the UN Sustainable Development Goals. Completion of primary and secondary education equips individuals with the needed skills and knowledge to establish businesses, seek employment, and save to secure their futures. Higher levels of education ultimately result in improved intergenerational mobility and sustained poverty reduction.

Ghana continues to face some challenges in this sector, including limited space for increased admission and insufficient infrastructure for senior high school education. In 2017, space constraints resulted in over 60,000, or 15% of Ghana's students, not being able to enrol in schools across the country, despite passing their Basic Education Certificate Examination to qualify.

Source: Authors paper

The government has made significant advances to improve education levels in the country, including the introduction of the Free Senior High School Policy to tackle challenges posed by financial constraints for students and their families.

This policy resulted in increased enrolment in public schools but worsened issues relating to seat or space inadequacy.

In response, multi-track year-round education was introduced, splitting the student body into separate tracks with a defined break-period rotation to boost school enrolment without expanding infrastructure. However, this policy increases maintenance and administrative costs and may even produce a negative effect on students' academic performance.

The government has since committed to building more schools to end the double-track system, raising considerable funds toward the required infrastructure investment.

But there is an alternative solution that shows strong potential to generate important cost savings. Because there is surplus capacity in the private school sector, providing subsidies for children to attend private schools will reduce the need and urgency to construct new schools.

Three researchers help inform us in the debate on expanding free senior high school education, Dr. Festus Ebo Turkson and Dr. Priscilla Twumasi Baffour of the Department of Economics, University of Ghana together with Dr. Brad Wong from Copenhagen Consensus. They estimate the costs and benefits of offering subsidies to those students who would enrol in private schools through the public placement system.

This involves helping families pay the cost of private secondary education with subsidies, with the target of enrolling 30,000 pupils per year. To keep costs down, the program would only subsidize students who could not secure a spot through the public placement system, which would require an annual transfer to parents of about GH₵ 60 million.

However, the investment in private schooling would alleviate the need to build 50 new public schools, saving the government GH₵ 250 million in infrastructure, as well as ongoing costs equal to GH₵ 60 million a year. This intervention would thus transfer the operating costs of the schooling from the public to the private sector while diverting the fixed costs of new school infrastructure to the future.

The researchers calculated the total cost of implementation at nearly GH₵ 500 million over 15 years, and the benefits at over GH₵ 730 million. Providing public subsidy to placement in private schools would thus generate a benefit 1.5 times higher than the original investment.

The potential learning benefits of this intervention would make the return on investment even more significant. Compared with the double-track system, public support may improve the quality of learning to all students enrolled in private schools, as these establishments could use the funds to support more teachers and better classroom inputs.

The researchers estimated the potential learning benefits in the form of test scores and future wages for the students to be significant as well, in the order of GHC 900 million. This would double the positive effect of the intervention, with every cedi spent on the initiative delivering over three cedis in social benefits.

These results are of crucial importance to help bring down the cost of free senior high schools while educating all qualified students and helping improve social mobility. Providing subsidies for pupils to attend private senior high school is likely to be a better investment than the alternative of building schools alone, especially at the present time.

In the context of coronavirus and a global recession, the government is even more pressed than usual to use resources in the smartest way possible, making the savings of GHC 250 million in school infrastructure and improved education all the more substantial.

Enrolling 30,000 new pupils per year over 15 years to private secondary education	**BCR**	**Benefit (GHC Million)**	**Cost (GHC Million)**
Provision of subsidies for private schooling with only operational and infrastructure benefits	1.5	734	491
Provision of subsidies with learning benefits incorporated	3.2	1,595	491

Total costs and benefits are discounted at 8%

Adding more Senior High School seats

Creating 30 000 new seats per grade requires

- **50 new school buildings**
  each costing GH¢ 50 million to construct
- **GH¢ 250 million**
  total construction cost
- **1800 students per school**
  total of 90 000 seats in 50 new schools
- **GH¢ 58.5 million**
  yearly operating cost corresponding to GH¢ 650 per student

Adding 30 000 seats per grade in existing private school

- **0 school buildings**
  utilise spare capacity in existing SHS
- **GH¢ 0 million**
  no construction needed
- **Add 300 new students per school**
  assuming 300 private SHS share 90 000 subsidised students equally
- **GH¢ 59 million**
  yearly cost of GH¢ 650 per student subsidy and administration
- **Learning spillover**
  slightly increased test scores for subsidised students

Total benefits and costs over 15 years

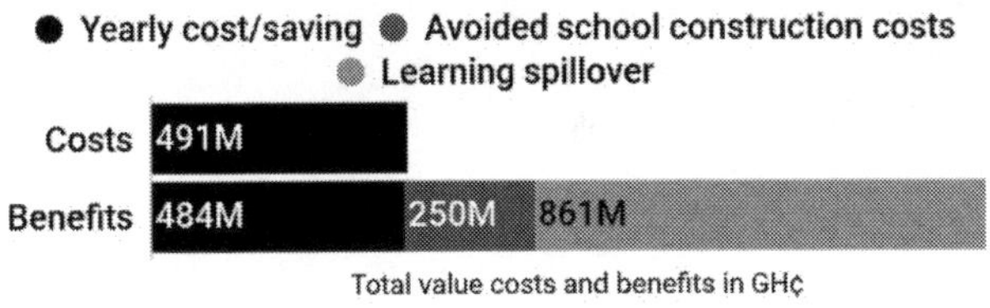

Source: Authors paper assuming 8% discount rate

Sanitation for a Cleaner and Healthier Future

Proper sanitation practices protect communities from diseases and maintain a clean and safe environment to promote the social, economic and physical wellbeing of the population.

In Ghana, liquid waste management has been largely neglected and remains an urgent issue with nationwide implications. In 2017, there were 41 million cases of diarrhoea and 7,300 related deaths in Ghana, much of it owing to poor sanitation. It has been estimated that as much as 88% of diarrhoeal disease in Accra and 75% of child deaths from cholera and diarrhoea in the country can be traced to this factor.

The economic burden is also considerable: in 2012, poor sanitation was estimated to have cost Ghana over $290 million, or 1.6% of GDP.

On-site sanitation systems, where full receptacles are collected and treated before discharging into the environment, are a common practice in Ghana, with a prevalence rate of over 85%. Unfortunately, there are few waste treatment plants and faecal sludge is typically dumped into water bodies, drains, trenches and other unauthorized places.

Faecal sludge treatment plants, when properly maintained and managed, can improve sanitation conditions and health outcomes. Several attempts have been made to rollout these facilities, but lack of skilled labour and resources for operation and maintenance has resulted in the plants remaining operational much less than their actual feasible operating lives.

New ideas are needed on the best ways to improve waste management, but with so many areas requiring the government's attention, prioritizing the initiatives with the biggest impact is crucial.

To target the urgent issue of correct sanitation practices, Esi Awuah, Ahmed Issahaku, Sampson Oduro-Kwarteng and

Micheal Addo Aziatsi from the Kwame Nkrumah University of Science and Technology, Martha Osei-Marfo from the University of Cape Coast, and Brad Wong of Copenhagen Consensus studied three interventions to improve liquid waste management: comprehensive treatment facilities, advanced stabilization ponds and resource recovery plants that convert waste into energy.

Comprehensive faecal sludge treatment plants remove settleable solids and improve the wastewater quality before it is reused, recycled or discharged into the environment. All generated sludge is pressed and can be used for biochar, activated carbon, or for processing sludge to electricity.

The researchers examined building 18 treatment plants in the large urban areas of all regions of Ghana. This intervention would reach 6.8 million people at the cost of GH₵ 1,350 million and help avoid 1.9 million cases of diarrhoea and 329 deaths in the first year.

Given that Ghana has a history of waste treatment plants gradually becoming non-operational due to lack of maintenance, the researchers also accounted for this in their calculation. Still, the total benefit would reach nearly GH₵ 4,000 million over the course of 15 years, meaning every cedi spent would yield a return nearly 3 times higher than the original investment.

The researchers also studied the cost-effectiveness of building traditional waste stabilization ponds for grit removal and effective disinfection. This intervention would be implemented in 46 locations across Ghana and would help avoid 1.9 million cases of diarrhoea and 263 deaths in the first year. The cost was estimated at GH₵ 930 million over 15 years, and the total benefits at GH₵ 4,100 million. Every cedi spent would yield benefits worth 4.4 cedis.

The researchers found resource recovery plants for converting biogas or sludge to electricity to be the most cost-effective solution. Building these plants across 64 locations throughout the country for the benefit of 14 million people was estimated to cost

GHC 1,400 million for sludge to energy and GHC 1,600 million for biogas to energy, but the estimated benefits are much higher.

As many as 3.8 million cases of diarrhoea and almost 600 deaths could be avoided in the first year, and the total economic benefits reach nearly GHC 7,500 million for each technology. Each cedi of investment would yield a return of around 5 cedis.

Poor end-of-pipe waste management poses a serious health challenge for Ghana, and better faecal sludge treatment technologies could significantly improve the quality of life for millions of Ghanaians.

Interventions	**BCR**	**Benefit (GHC Million)**	**Cost (GHC Million)**
Sludge to energy	5.3	7,451	1,395
Biogas to energy	4.7	7,485	1,579
Stabilization ponds	4.4	4,113	926
Comprehensive treatment plans	2.9	3,962	1,349

Total costs and benefits are discounted at 8%

Comprehensive FSTP for Kumasi by PURECO of Hungary
(Source: Authors paper)

Sludge Biomass to Electricity
(Source: Authors paper)

Equal Access to Health Care

Ghanaians' health issues have shifted over time, from infectious diseases and maternal and child health problems to ever more non-communicable diseases. The current co-existence of diseases like malaria and tuberculosis with hypertension, stroke and diabetes presents a challenge for the country's health care system, and especially for the poor.

Households living in poverty can experience catastrophic healthcare expenditures, live in less sanitary environments, and may lack the participatory power to change their community and health systems. The situation is even more critical in the rural communities of the three northern regions, with only one doctor for every 20,000 people.

While 82% of mothers in urban Ghana have access to skilled birth attendants for delivery, the proportion is only 43% in rural zones, where nearly half the population resides.

In order to improve access to health care, Nkechi S. Owoo and Monica P. Lambon-Quayefio from the University of Ghana and Brad Wong from Copenhagen Consensus studied the impact of expanding health insurance, operating and maintaining ambulance networks in rural zones, and incentivising health care workers to move to remote areas.

Today, only about 62% of poor households have health insurance, despite the implementation of the National Health Insurance Scheme (NHIS). The premiums and enrolment fee often serve as a deterrent for extremely poor households, and the poorest communities have limited facilities and opportunities for seeking care.

The researchers studied the potential impact of identifying and enrolling the remaining 2.7 million poor into the NHIS system, as well as abolishing the user fees and annual premium payments for all poor and transferring the cost to the insured non-poor. Over a 10-year period, the total costs of the intervention would reach nearly GH₵ 6 billion, but greater use of health services could bring improved health and a significant reduction of mortality. Over 1,700 deaths could be avoided annually, and the economic benefits, including the value of free insurance, would be more than double the costs, at GHȻ 12 billion.

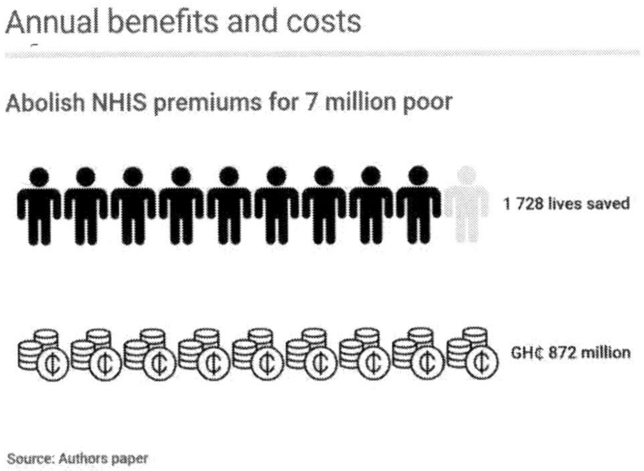

An efficient ambulance system also plays a critical role in reducing disease and death, but the lack of access to emergency health care is common in rural areas. Patients requiring emergency care are transported to health facilities on bicycles, motorbikes or carts driven by animals, which increases the risk of complications.

In January 2020, the government distributed over 300 ambulances across the country, and the researchers analysed the costs and benefits of continuing to maintain and operate this emergency care network in rural Ghana. They estimated the total cost of the intervention, including the construction of ambulance stations, at GHȻ 650 million.

The benefit is the avoidance of 218 maternal and 1,100 intrapartum deaths as well as 600 deaths from trauma and injury avoided annually, amounting to an economic benefit of over GHȻ 13 billion for the 10-year period. Every cedi spent on this initiative would yield a return over 20 times higher than the original investment.

Annual benefits and costs

Maintain and operate rural ambulance network

Source: Authors paper

Adequate delivery of health care would be difficult without an adequate health workforce, but staffing rural facilities is challenging. In Ghana, the southern half of the country attracts most of the trained health staff, which leads to inequitable distribution of professionals. The researchers assessed the cost-effectiveness of providing incentives to attract and retain health workers in deprived areas, including a 30% salary increase, guaranteed comfortable accommodation, and an education scholarship.

Increasing the base salary would cost around GH₵ 2 million per year and incentivise 44 more doctors to work in the three northern regions of the country, helping save 75 lives and bringing in GH₵ 60 million in economic benefits. Providing superior housing, in turn, would cost GH₵ 13 million per year and attract 207 more doctors to work in the rural north, for a benefit of over GH₵ 280 million, including 357 avoided deaths.

An education scholarship would cost GH₵ 5 million per year and incentivize 76 more doctors to work in the remote north, with the potential of saving 131 lives and generating a benefit of over

GHC 100 million. Every cedi spent on these incentives would create benefits between 21 and 26 cedis.

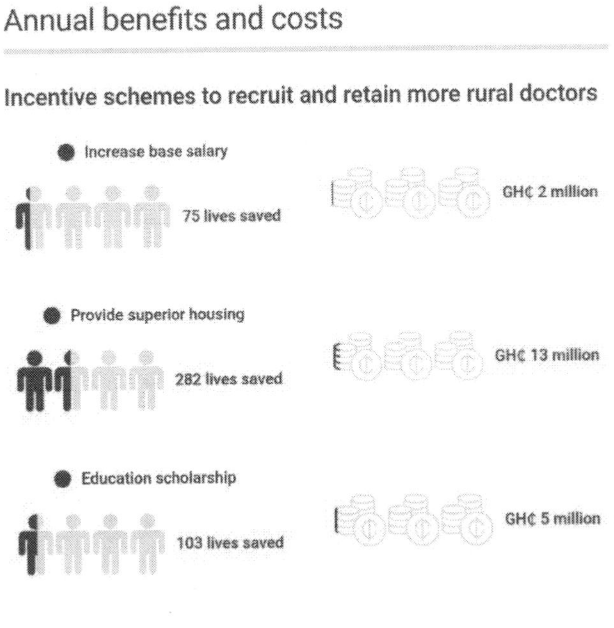

Source: Authors paper

Both the maintenance of the ambulance system and incentives for relocation could greatly benefit the rural population. Access to health care services is essential to achieving national goals of universal health coverage and equity, and together these cost-effective interventions can pave the way for a healthier future for Ghana.

Value for money (benefit-cost ratios)

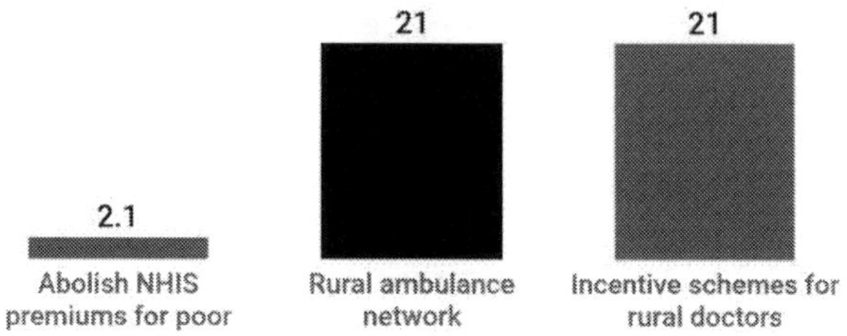

Interventions	BCR	Annualized Benefit (millions of GH₵)	Annualized Cost (millions of GH₵)
Incentive schemes			
Salary top-ups	25.8	59	2
Housing	21.0	282	13
Education scholarship	20.8	103	5
Maintain an emergency transportation systems in rural communities	20.6	1,981	96
NHIS Premium subsidy	2.1	1,814	872

Total costs and benefits are discounted at 8%

The Smartest Ways to Save Mothers and Infants

The infant and maternal mortality are important indicators of a nation's wellbeing and the overall quality of its health system. Over the last three decades, Ghana has achieved much improved primary care for mothers and children, but mortality rates are still significantly higher than the targets of the UN Sustainable Development Goals.

Most deaths that occur during the first days or months of life could be avoided. Complications caused by pre-term birth and infections are among the largest causes of mortality in the first month, and children under five are most vulnerable to preventable diseases such as malaria and diarrhea.

Most maternal deaths for infections, high blood pressure and complications related to birth could also be averted. However, remote rural zones often lack basic health care coverage and expanding new initiatives is costly. How can decision-makers reduce these risks, while using limited resources in the smartest way possible?

Patrick Opoku Asuming and Edmund Wedam Kanmiki of the University of Ghana and Brad Wong of Copenhagen Consensus studied the effect of scaling up three strategic health systems interventions that have brought great results for maternal and child health: the Ghana Essential Health Intervention Program (GEHIP) implemented in Northern Ghana, the NEWborn Health INTervention Study (NEWHINTS) undertaken in the middle belt, and ensuring access to emergency obstetric and neonatal care.

GEHIP was a five-year trial launched in 2010, designed to strengthen the health systems in remote locations by expanding community-based primary healthcare and improving leadership capacity at the district level. Together with providing medicines and vaccines, GEHIP places the focus on training health care providers and promoting community engagement. The program achieved incredible results, reaching 6.8% of Ghana's rural population and reducing neonatal deaths in these areas significantly.

The *Ghana Priorities* research shows that expanded to include 100% of Ghana's rural population, GEHIP would reduce neonatal mortality by 10% on average over 7 years saving the lives of 7,551 newborn children. The cost of the intervention would be GH₵ 159 million, while the economic and social benefits would be worth GH₵ 6.1 billion. This means scaling up GEHIP would bring a return 38 times higher than the original investment.

The NEWHINTS intervention, on the other hand, included training health workers to identify pregnant women in their communities and to perform home visits during pregnancy and the first week after birth. The goal was to improve delivery and care practices for mothers and newborn babies, and in the trial, the program was found to reduce neonatal mortality by 8%.

According to the study, an expansion of NEWHINTS to cover 100% of Ghana's rural population would help save 819 newborn lives every year. At the cost of GH₵ 24.9 million, the initiative would bring GH₵ 698 million worth of social benefit annually. Every cedi spent on NEWHINTS would bring social and economic benefits worth 28 cedis.

Improving access to emergency obstetric and neonatal care is also recommended for rural locations poor in resources to reduce infant and maternal mortality. The analysis took into account existing hospitals and other health care facilities that lack the capacity to provide these services, and calculated the cost of filling the logistical and human needs, including minor renovations of already existing buildings. This intervention was calculated to achieve a 27% reduction in mortality during birth.

The projected economic benefits of implementing this initiative in the whole country over 15 years were estimated at GH₵ 4.6 billion and the costs at GH₵ 838 million, meaning every cedi spent would create 5.6 cedis worth of social good.

The researchers found the interventions to be valuable tools for reducing infant and maternal mortality, but the important success recorded with GEHIP underlines the need for a comprehensive, holistic approach. The combination of leadership and community support, improved training of health service employees, and extra focus on newborn surveillance and care have been proven to have a major impact on mortality rates.

This study provides the government with useful opportunities for strengthening the health system and effectively saving lives across the country.

Interventions	BCR	Benefit (GHC Million)	Cost (GHC Million)
Ghana Essential Health Interventions Program (GEHIP)	38	6,149 over 6 years	159 over 6 years
NEWHINTS home visits	28	698 per year	24.8 per year
Emergency Obstretric and Neonatal Care (EmONC)	5.6	4,647 over 15 years	836 over 15 years

Total costs and benefits are discounted at 8%

Interventions saving mothers and infants

Social value for money (benefit-cost ratio)

1. **38x GEHIP**
   expand community-based primary healthcare and improve leadership capacity at the district level would cost GH¢ 159 million over 6 years

2. **28x NEWHINTS**
   improve delivery and care practices would cost GH¢ 25 million per year

3. **5.6x EmONC**
   improve access to emergency obstetric and neonatal care for 100% of Ghana's rural population would cost GH¢ 838 million over 15 years

Source: Authors' computations using 8% discount rate

Cleaner Air for Every Household

Cooking over an open fire or with traditional stoves is widely practiced in Ghana, but these common methods carry serious risks. Emissions caused by the use of solid fuels such as wood, coal, and charcoal are one of the leading health concerns in many developing countries.

Globally, over 1.6 million people died in 2017 from diseases related to poor household air quality, and in Ghana, 10,000 lives are lost to this cause annually.

As much as 78% of the population relies on charcoal and wood as primary cooking fuels and only 21% use liquefied petroleum gas (LPG), a much cleaner cooking method. Reliance on solid fuels is even greater in rural areas because of the large distances to refill stations: while 35% of people in urban settings use LPG, the same is only true for 6% of the rural population.

Using solid cooking fuels also affects surrounding households, given that smoke is vented out, which pollutes the outdoor air. All of this makes improved cooking methods an important public health issue that should be addressed now that Ghana is on a path of continuous economic growth and development.

To reduce the use of harmful cooking methods in Ghana, Maxwell Dalaba from the Navrongo Health Research Centre, independent consultant Bjorn Larsen, and Brad Wong from Copenhagen Consensus evaluated the costs and benefits of three policy interventions to improve household air quality for all Ghanaians: cylinder recirculation and a new distribution system of LPG in rural areas, elimination of taxes on LPG, and promotion of improved fuelwood and charcoal cookstoves.

In rural Ghana, clean cooking fuels are often difficult to access. The study estimates that for rural Ghanaians, having to travel to refill stations effectively increases the costs of LPG by 50%. The researchers studied the effect of introducing a cylinder recirculation model, which would enable operators to transport LPG cylinders from the city so that they can be sold in local stores in rural areas. The initiative would expand the proportion of the rural population using clean cooking fuels from 6% to 17%, equivalent to nearly 800,000 households.

This would save 181 lives per year and deliver economic benefits from fuel savings along with reduced cooking and travelling time. The benefits are worth almost GH₵ 5,000 per household over ten-years. The costs are estimated at GH₵ 2,300 per household, mostly in the form of LPG fuel. This means every cedi spent on this initiative would bring a return twice as high in social and economic benefits.

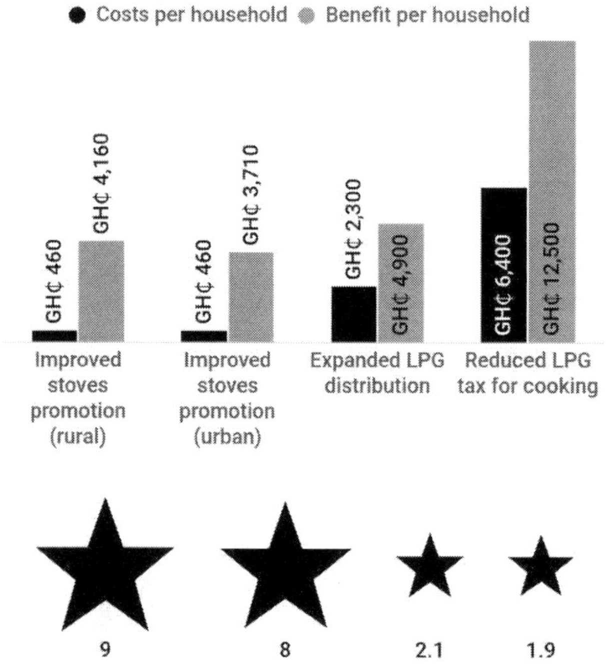

Value for money (benefit-cost ratio)

The researchers also studied the effect of removing the 23% value-added tax, which serves to reduce the affordability and use of LPG. The intervention would lead to 391,000 urban households and 80,000 rural households switching to LPG.

This change, in turn, would help reduce deaths by 193 per year, while delivering significant time and fuel savings for the beneficiaries. The health improvements, savings and reduced cooking time are estimated to be worth GH₵ 12,500 per household over 10 years. However, the intervention would cost GH₵ 6,400 per household, including lost government revenues of nearly GH₵ 190m annually. Overall, the initiative would generate benefits 1.9 times higher than the original investment.

The researchers finally investigated the effect of changing from traditional cookstoves or open fire to improved, more energy-efficient clean cook stoves that generate less smoke. They found that if 565,000 households switched to improved stoves, 186 deaths would be avoided per year.

The savings made in fuel, time and improved health for this initiative are estimated to be between GH₵ 2,700 and 6,100 per household, 6 to 13 times the modest initial investment of GH₵ 460 per beneficiary.

Promotion of improved charcoal and fuelwood cookstoves delivers the highest benefits from each cedi spent and it is a good intermediate solution, thanks to its low cost. LPG or other clean cooking solutions can deliver larger health benefits per household, but at much higher costs. Overall, these initiatives offer decision-makers valuable new options to effectively improve air quality and save lives.

Benefits and costs per household

Interventions		BCR	Benefit (GH₵ Million)	Cost (GH₵ Million)
Promotion of improved wood stove	national	6-13	2,700 -6,100	460
Expanded distribution of LPG in rural areas	rural	2.1	4,900	2,300
Elimination on taxes on LPG for cooking	national	1.9	12,500	6,400

Total costs and benefits are discounted at 8%

HYPERTENSION - GHANA'S DISEASE OF THE FUTURE?

In Ghana, health care policy interventions and research budgets have traditionally been directed towards combatting communicable diseases like HIV/AIDS, malaria and tuberculosis. These are still a major public health concern, but as the country advances toward greater prosperity, the prevalence of non-communicable diseases is also rapidly increasing.

Cardiovascular diseases, cancers and diabetes are particularly on the rise in Ghana, and one of the largest risk factors for complications such as stroke and coronary heart disease is high blood pressure. The number of people suffering from hypertension increases every year, and it has become one of the most rapidly growing risk factors for disease over the last decade.

Hypertension has been estimated to affect around 13% of working-age people in the country, and the condition is significantly more prevalent in urban areas.

Hypertension awareness and treatment levels are also very low, which increases the risk of further health complications. It has been estimated that 63% of women and 86% of men with high blood pressure in Ghana are unaware of their condition, and amongst the hypertensive patients only 17% of women and 6% of men had treated and controlled their high blood pressure.

Ghana only has one doctor per every 7000 patients, which makes diagnosing conditions such as hypertension more difficult. This situation can be improved by shifting some primary care duties, like managing high blood pressure, to non-physician health care workers, and only referring high-risk cases to doctors.

Still, more needs to be done on prevention to lower the overall incidence of hypertension and reduce the risks of the serious diseases it leads to.

Decision-makers in Ghana have taken note of this growing challenge and several interventions have been tested in the past to improve awareness and treatment of hypertension, but it's difficult to design effective public health policies without comprehensive information. Resources are always limited, so it's crucial to know exactly where every cedi of public investment would do the most good.

Dr. Emmanuel Ekow Asmah and Dr. Francis K. Andoh from the University of Cape Coast and Dr. Saleema Razvi and Dr. Brad Wong of Copenhagen Consensus examined the impact of screening and treating hypertension.

They calculated the costs and benefits of screening 2.5 million people aged 30 and above for hypertension and other cardiovascular disease risk factors. The intervention would be performed by community health workers visiting households, and individuals with high blood pressure would be referred to a health facility for further assessment and, if necessary, placed on medication. Over time, doctors would manage those with the most severe hypertension, with the rest relying on community health workers.

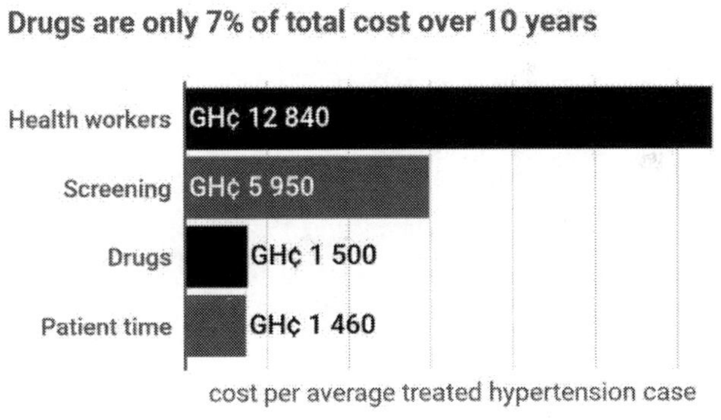

Source: Authors paper

The researchers estimated the cost of this intervention would be GH₵ 220 million over a 10 year period. Two thirds of this cost would be for the on-going visits to the doctor or health worker. Screening for hypertension, including time and travel costs for the patients would cost GH₵ 60 million, with only GH₵ 10 million for the medication.

Result of screening 2.5 million over 30 years old

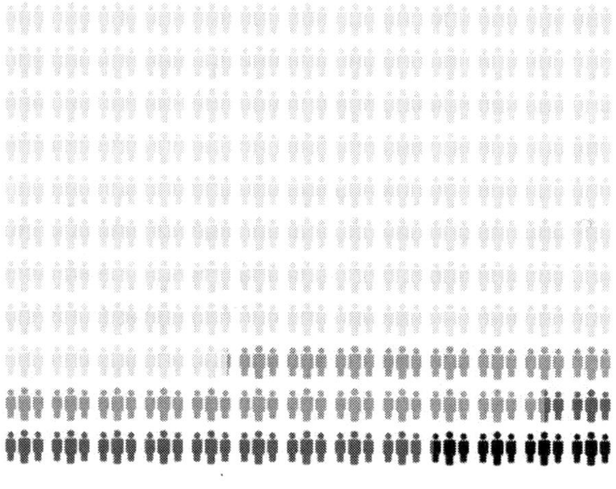

Healthy ● Referred to doctor ● Start treatment

● Stay on treatment 5 or more years

Source: Authors paper

Based on population surveys, more than 250,000 new cases of hypertension would be found, some 230,000 would start medication and 30% would still continue their treatment after five years. 2900 deaths and 1100 cases of heart disease could be avoided, adding up to about 50,000 life years saved. Over ten years, the total benefits would be larger than GH₵ 700 million. Every cedi spent would yield more than 3 cedis in social and economic benefits.

While such screening and treatment could be a cost-effective use of resources to combat hypertension, Ghana's current health challenges still skew heavily towards causes like malaria, nutrition, maternal and child health.

Crucially, the Ghana Priorities project has shown that many policy interventions in these areas have benefit-cost ratios many times higher, with each cedi spent on tuberculosis treatment yielding up to 190 cedis in benefits to society, or 134 cedis in the case of malaria. Clearly, most scarce resources should first be prioritized on these policies that will help the most people most effectively.

Value for money

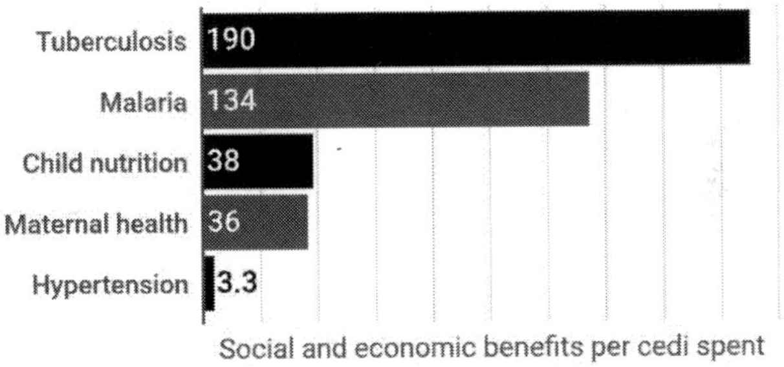

Source: Authors paper, and other Ghana Priorities papers assuming 8% discount rate

Still, beginning to focus on hypertension makes sense in two ways. First, it is still a worthwhile — though not amazing — use of resources. Second, as Ghana develops further and gets infectious diseases under control, hypertension will become an ever more relevant problem. It is therefore worth revisiting this analysis and policy implications once progress has been made on today's urgent health challenges.

Costs and benefits of tackling hypertension over a 10-year period

	BCR	Benefit (GH₵ Million)	Cost (GH₵ Million)
Community health worker-led screening and treatment of 2.5 million people	3.3	710	220

Total costs and benefits are discounted at 8%

Protecting Ghana's Artisanal Mining Sector

Proper Artisanal and small-scale gold mining (ASM) is an important economic activity that has provided jobs and supported the livelihoods of many rural Ghanaian communities for over a century. While the country implemented mineral sector reforms in the 1980s to attract foreign direct investment into the large-scale mining sector, the contribution of ASM to total gold production has been steadily rising, as well.

In 1989, it accounted for about 2% of the sector's output. By 2018, the figure rose to 41%.

The sector does, however, face some struggles. While an estimated 1.1 million people are currently engaged in this activity, 60% of them are illegal or unregistered. Bureaucratic bottlenecks and prohibitive licensing costs drive miners to illegal operations, and favouritism towards large-scale operators has come at the expense of small-scale miners.

ASM also has numerous negative social and environmental effects in Ghana. In the quest to minimize production costs, some artisanal miners use harmful technologies that negatively affect the health of those involved, and miners are often exposed to injuries and death resulting from cave-ins of mine shafts.

The obsolete technologies also lead to significant environmental damages, including land and rainforest degradation and mercury pollution of water bodies. For example, alluvial gold mining operations have been found to pollute over 200 water bodies within mining districts in Ghana. Mining operations damage riverbanks and divert streams from their natural courses, contributing to the incidence of floods and resulting in irreversible damages to ecosystems.

The contribution of ASM to economic development and transformation can no longer be ignored. Designing the right policies can help improve the miners' conditions and prevent environmental degradation, but decision-makers need to ensure they invest scarce public resources in the most cost-effective policies.

To help mitigate the negative impact of ASM operations in Ghana's, Wisdom Akpalu from the Ghana Institute of Management and Public Administration (GIMPA) and the Environment and Natural Resource Research Initiative in Ghana (ENRRI-EfD Ghana), and Brad Wong of Copenhagen Consensus focused on the costs and benefits of establishing mining co-operatives.

These associations support mining activities from extraction to commercialization, and in many countries, have proven to be an effective way of formalizing small-scale mining to adopt improved technologies, increase efficiency, reduce environmental impacts and minimize social conflicts.

To make mining co-operatives a part of the formalization of ASM operations in Ghana, the Ministry of Mines, in consultation with the Minerals Commission, can designate an area for small scale mining, especially targeting unregistered miners. The researchers estimated the need to register 1120 co-operatives in 40 mining districts, each consisting of 590 ASM operators. These co-operative unions would be granted a mineralized land to be mined for five years at a time.

The cost related to the establishment of mining co-operatives includes the cost of setting up and sensitizing mining communities to the opportunities of co-operatives. It also takes into account the operational cost of using improved technologies, as miners switch from manual to mechanized tools.

The government would also need to support and incentivize co-operatives by providing grants, which the researchers estimate at GH₵ 216 million per year. Over 10 years, the total cost of the intervention is GH₵ 7 billion, borne both by the government and the cooperatives.

As for the benefits, easing the formalization process and constituting co-operatives makes it easier for members to pool their skills and financial resources together, acquire innovative technologies and increase their output and earnings. The use of improved mining methods also promotes cleaner gold production and reduces the significant environmental damages of mining, as well as the risk of accidents, mortality and in-utero exposure to mercury from harmful production practices.

Mining co-operatives' financial model of shared savings can also result in greater capital accumulation, generating total benefits worth nearly GHC 8.3 billion. While the overall cost of this intervention is high, every cedi spent would create 1.2 cedis of social good.

Mining co-operatives are a community-based management strategy that could help legally formalize collective decision-making and sharing of responsibilities and generate significant social returns. Through this intervention, the government can help miners improve their technologies and scale up production while taking better care of their health and the environment.

Intervention	**BCR**	**Benefit (GHC Million)**	**Cost (GHC Million)**
Establishment of mining co-operatives	1.2	8,265	7,040

Total costs and benefits are discounted at 8%

Artisanal mining cooperatives

Estimated costs of formalising small-scale mining

Sensitisation and set-up

500,000 per cooperative would add up to GHS 562 million

Improved mining technology

510,000 per cooperative would add up to GHS 574 million annually

Grant incentives to miners

192,000 per cooperative would add up to GHS 216 million per year

Administrative

162,000 per cooperative of mining concession fees, office and utilities costs, and monitoring and evaluation adding up to GHS 182 million per year

Resulting economic, social & environmental benefits

Improved production

593,000 per operator would add up to GHS 664 million per year

Grant incentives to miners

192,000 per cooperative adding up to GHS 216 million per year is transferred to the miners and therefore also a benefit

Less environmental degradation

Improved biodiversity, and increased water for household and industrial consumption valued at GHS 136 million per year

Fewer accidents and injuries

5 lives saved per year, 86,000 abrasions, 28,000 fractures, and 76,000 lacerations avoided valued at GHS 132 million per year

Avoided mercury exposure in utero

Each year roughly 47,190 children would be born to the beneficiary population with an annual benefit of GHS 64 million

Source: Authors' paper

INDUSTRIAL TRANSFORMATIONS FOR GROWTH AND DEVELOPMENT

Even with Ghana's impressive economic growth in recent times, the country's industries still lag behind the services sector in its contribution to both GDP and employment. Ghanaian manufacturers struggle to overcome the difficulties posed by infrastructure problems, informality, and the lack of skilled labour and good management practices.

Financial constraints, high cost of doing business and difficulties to access credit also make growth harder for companies of all sizes.

Ghana needs to build up its industry to promote overall growth for the long term. The government can help catalyse this transformation, but public resources are limited, and it is often difficult to assess where increased spending would do the most for overall development and wellbeing.

To transform Ghana's industrial sector, Prof. Peter Quartey, Dr. Festus Ebo Turkson, Daniel Chachu and Mawuenyega Makafui Butu from the University of Ghana together with Emmanuel Abbey from the African Universities Alliance analysed a series of interventions designed to improve profitability, economic growth, and employment.

Improving management is one solution. A survey of 33 nations finds Ghana's average managerial score close to the bottom. But several studies show that if government pays for consulting services, it can significantly improve factory operations and processes in areas such as quality control, human resources, inventory, and sales.

The average costs and benefits for medium-sized companies are based on a randomized controlled study in Kumasi, and for large companies it relies on similar data from India. The cost for management consulting is GH₵ 1.6 million per large company and GH₵ 7,000 for medium-sized companies. But such management training can help businesses to grow and become more profitable.

International comparison of management quality

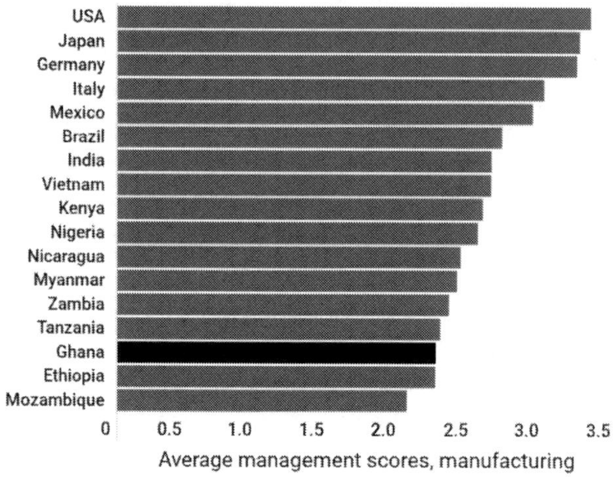

Source: Author's paper (Bloom, Sadun and Van Reenen)

It can increase Ghanaian profits in larger companies by GH₵ 10.5 million for the initial 6 years. For medium-sized companies, the benefits of consulting in the first year alone were estimated at GH₵ 71,000. Every cedi spent by the government on improving management practices would thus bring a return 6 times higher than the original investment for large enterprises, and almost 10 times higher for medium-sized companies.

Consulting could also have a spillover effect on other local firms that would see their growth and productiveness increase by implementing these improved management practices.

Access to credit is another crucial factor for private businesses and economies. Financing for companies could be promoted in Ghana by ensuring better surveillance of the credit referencing system, better address systems, improving the quality of information available to lenders and enforcing a rewards and sanctions regime.

Better information reduces risks for lenders, and as a result more credit becomes available at a lower interest rate. This would help Ghanaian companies make the necessary investments to grow and improve. The researchers discovered that the provision of better information in the credit system would cost GHȻ 6 million per year, but the benefits in credit availability and cost could reach GHȻ 70 million per year.

Every cedi spent would create nearly 12 cedis worth of benefits to society.

Private sector credit as percentage of GDP

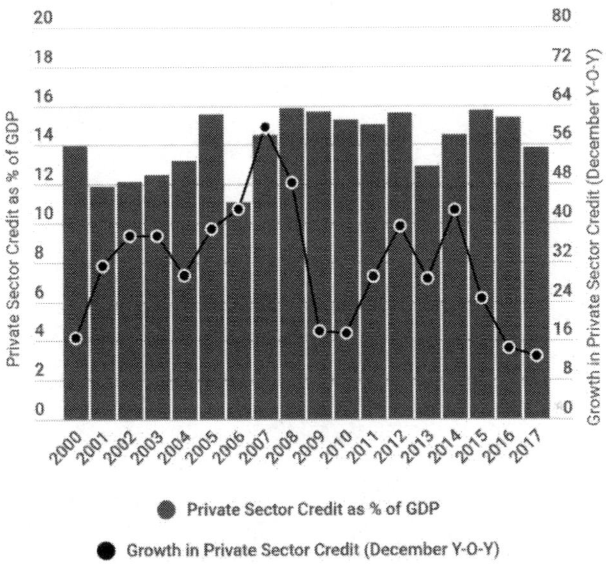

Source: World Development Indicators and Bank of Ghana database (24th June 2019)

The researchers also looked at doubling public spending dedicated to research and development from 0.4% to 0.8% of GDP, or by GHȻ 1.2 billion. Investment in R&D has been one of the most important sources of economic growth in many developed countries in recent times, and it could have a big impact on Ghana's industrial sector. Every cedi spent could generate benefits worth 1.5 to 1.75 cedis, boosting economic growth by at least 0.6 percentage points per year if spending on R&D is doubled.

The manufacturing sector could also receive a significant boost from grants to small businesses and from reducing the cost of electricity for industries. The researchers found that subsidies for electricity could create profits for the companies worth 1.8 times the original investment, while providing capital grants to selected microenterprises were estimated to generate a benefit of 7 cedis for every cedi spent.

In conclusion, industrial transformation has been the main source of growth and employment creation for many advanced economies. In order to maintain and increase the promising levels of growth of recent years and provide wellbeing for all its citizens, Ghana needs to transform its industrial sector structurally.

These interventions could point the way to the implementation of Ghana's current 10-Point Industrialization Strategy which when well implemented, could provide the much-needed development for the long term.

Interventions	**BCR**	**Benefit per firm (GHC Million)**	**Cost per firm (GHC Million)**
Credit reference bureau	11.7	69	5.9
Management training for medium-sized firms	9.6	65,726	6,876
Management consultants for large manufacturing enterprises	5.9	9,581,100	1,163,400

Interventions	BCR	Benefit per year (GHC Million)	Cost per year (GHC Million)
Capital grant for micro enterprises	7.0	5,263	752
Reduce industrial electricity tariff	1.8	988	534
Doubled general R&D Spending	1.5	1800	1200

Total costs and benefits are discounted at 8%

Value for money (benefit-cost ratio)

1 — 12x Access to credit

More and cheaper credit for borrowers through expansion of the current credit referencing system to include data from fintechs, mining companies, wholesalers, court records and tax records

2 — 6-10x Improved management

Large manufacturing firms are likely to benefit much **more from the management training relative to medium-sized firms, though the** costs of assisting large firms to enhance their profits are obviously much higher.

3 — 7x Grants for micro-enterprises

In-kind asset transfer (752 GHC per beneficiary) to increase the profitability of microenterprises given the difficulty they face in raising funds at a reasonable cost

4 — 1.8x Industrial electricity tariff

A lower tariff for industry increases the use of electricity for manufacturing creating leading to an increase in value-add and output.

5 — 1.5 -1.75x Doubled R&D spending

Although supporting infrastructure to take advantage of returns to R&D investments is absent, some productivity improvements are still envisaged.

Source: Author's paper

Land Title Reform for Increased Investment, Security and Development

Ghana's economy has shown robust growth in the past two decades, with GDP per capita increasing by 88% in real terms during this period. Still, poverty remains a challenge, especially among the rural population.

For an economy largely reliant on agriculture and mineral resource mining like Ghana's, land plays a crucial role in development. However, the land structure in the country is complicated, with most holdings remaining in customary ownership, untitled, and undocumented. This generates problems of disputes and inadequate utilization of the property.

The formalization of land rights through titling has positive implications for investments, land productivity, and socioeconomic development in general.

Increase in property values after land titling

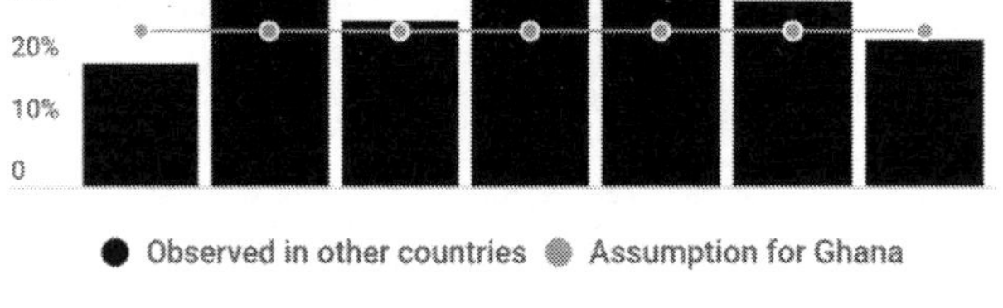

Source: Authors paper

Titling is a crucial step in providing assurance for ownership and securing investments. Security to land streamlines transactions and greatly increases the propensity to invest with a long-term perspective. Well-documented private property rights also facilitate the use of land as collateral for loans and therefore provide easier access to credit. Given all these benefits, it is not surprising that registered title has been found to raise property values by as much as 60%.

Some major reforms, policies and laws have been implemented in the last three decades both in Ghana and globally. However, due to the magnitude of the challenges in titling in Ghana, a lot remains to be done to register the majority of holdings and enhance the effectiveness of the system.

If conditions are right, well-implemented land registration programs can help improve governance and administrative efficiency, reduce the need to spend resources on enforcing land rights, enhance gender equality, increase land-related investment, and enhance the operation of land markets as well as credit access.

Spending resources for land title reform can drive development in Ghana, but public resources are always limited, and identifying the areas where investment would do the most good is crucial.

To provide Ghana with a modern land records database as the foundation for smoother transactions and economic growth, Charles Adjasi from the Stellenbosch University in South Africa, Stanislaus Adiaba from the Lands Commission of Ghana, and Brad Wong and Saleema Razvi of Copenhagen Consensus studied the possibility of surveying and documenting over more than half of Ghana's land area — 170,000 square kilometres of customary lands in Ghana to build a comprehensive and automated national base land map.

The intervention would require updating and modernizing the existing national base map, surveying and demarcation of customary land ownership, and rehabilitating the Continuously Operating Referencing Station (CORS) network, a system of about 200 stations across the country.

It would also include the digitization of documents and automation of the registration process, as well as a national awareness campaign to sensitize citizenry, traditional rulers and families about the intervention. A new legal and arbitration framework would be needed to resolve disputes and review previous court judgments, possibly through engagement with the National and Regional House of Chiefs and a committee of eminent judges, statespersons and land administrators.

The researchers estimated the total cost of these components of the land reform programme at GHC 940 million.

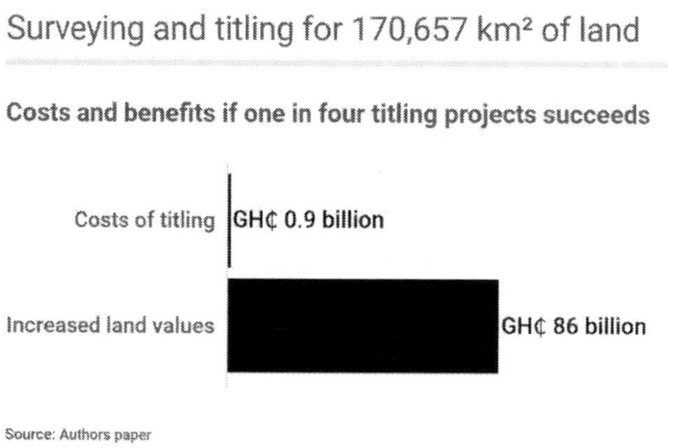

While the costs are high, there are many benefits associated with land titling, including improved access to credit, higher certainty for investments and smoother land transactions. One of the clearest and largest advantages is the increased property value of titled land, estimated at 25%. However, land-titling reform is not a simple endeavour. Given the challenges of previous land reform in Ghana and around the world, the researchers conservatively assumed that any project would only have a 25% likelihood of actually working. Even then, the total benefits were estimated around GHC 86,123 million. Every cedi spent on the reform would yield a benefit of around 90 cedis.

International experience shows that land reform is likely to be a lengthy process and the probability of success depends on the appropriate legal structures, adequate appreciation of the customary issues related to land, and the extent of political support behind the intervention.

When successful, land reform eliminates barriers to increase sustainability and has numerous favourable outcomes for social, economic, and political development. This recent study truly gives Ghanaian policymakers interesting new inputs for the discussion on economic growth and poverty reduction through a modernized, automated land registry and increased security for investments.

Intervention	BCR	Benefit (GH₵ Million)	Cost (GH₵ Million)
Survey and documentation of 170,657 square kilometres of land at a 25% success rate.	91	86,123	942

Total costs and benefits are discounted at 8%

THE SMARTEST WAYS TO FIGHT MALARIA

Healthy societies are productive societies, and Ghana is making great progress. In many areas, from improved nutrition and poverty reduction to disease prevention, the country is witnessing significant development. However, malaria remains a major public health concern. With one of every five citizens affected every year, it is the leading cause of death and disease and a great toll on all of society.

Malaria places an enormous demand on the country's health system and decreases productivity, with an estimated annual economic burden of 1% to 2% of GDP. Of all workdays lost in Ghana, 40% are due to malaria, and 13.5% of individuals in the prime working ages between 15 and 49 contract it annually.

An increase in malaria incidence of 1% has been shown to reduce economic growth by 0.41%, and the regions most affected by it have a much slower rate of development than the national average.

Malaria prevention and treatment methods have made great advances in the past decades, and new research can point to the most cost-effective measures.

In the fight against malaria, where should resources be increased first to reap the biggest social benefit?

Edward Nketiah-Amponsah from the University of Ghana, Timothy Awine and Sheetal Silal from the University of Cape Town, and Brad Wong from Copenhagen Consensus studied the best current initiatives to limit the spread of the disease.

They calculated the benefit of scaling up three strategies already in use: diagnostic testing of suspected malaria cases at health facilities, distribution of insecticide-treated bed nets, and seasonal malaria chemoprevention.

For years, the government has prioritized increasing the use of bed nets to prevent the spread of the disease, with great results.

The first analysed initiative expects to increase the number of bed nets distributed, with the goal of reaching 90% coverage in 2023 and maintaining it thereafter. This would require extra funding for the National Malaria Control Program (NMCP) of 45 million GH₵ initially, with a total cost of ₵442 million by 2030.

Bed nets are relatively inexpensive, but making coverage near-universal would have a big impact: 12.9 million cases of uncomplicated malaria, some 700,000 severe cases, and 40,000 deaths could be avoided in the time frame studied. The total social and economic benefits would be 44 times the original investment, at about 19,000 million GH₵.

Among the initiatives analysed, increasing testing to confirm suspected malaria cases in health facilities would bring the highest benefits for every cedi spent. Testing is currently targeted at 90% of cases and helps limit indiscriminate use of anti-malarial treatment, which saves money and protects the public through more accurate diagnoses.

The study investigates an increase towards near-universal implementation by training health facility staff in the use of the right protocols and making improvements in the availability of equipment, as well as monitoring.

Reaching the last 10% of coverage would be significantly more difficult than the previous expansion of testing, with the authors estimating that reaching these last cases would be 10 times as costly per suspected patient compared to what Ghana has paid so far.

Even with these large extra costs, the return on investment from this intervention would be massive. By properly diagnosing malaria and giving early treatment to those infected, 435,000 severe cases and close to 25,000 deaths could be avoided between now and 2030. The study also suggests savings in drugs and time worth around GH₵ 17 for every suspected malaria case. The total value of benefits by 2030 would be a phenomenal GH₵ 11,600 million. Every cedi spent would create benefits worth GH₵134.

Young children are the most vulnerable to malaria. Seasonal malaria chemoprevention targeted at children up to five years of age is another strategy that has brought good results for the NMCP. The researchers considered increasing preventive treatment in the Guinea Savannah region to 90%, to bring preventive medicine to up to 600,000 children.

This would require significant planning and human resources, but in total would help save more than 3,000 lives by 2030. The total benefit is calculated at GH₵ 2,300 million and the costs at GH₵ 167 million, meaning each cedi produces GH₵ 14 in social benefits — still a very respectable return.

Investments to ramp up malaria initiatives can be a very good way forward for Ghana, not only in saving lives but in achieving higher productivity for the future. This study can help the Health Ministry spend extra resources to do the most good for Ghana.

Interventions	**BCR**	**Benefit (GH₵ Million)**	**Cost (GH₵ Million)**
Distribute and sustain 90 per cent coverage of LLIN	44	19,359	442
Seasonal Malaria Chemoprevention to 90 per cent of children in the Guinea Savannah zone	14	2,303	167
Near universal coverage of testing and treatment at health facilities	134	11,595	87

Total costs and benefits are discounted at 8%

Comparing malaria initiatives scale-up

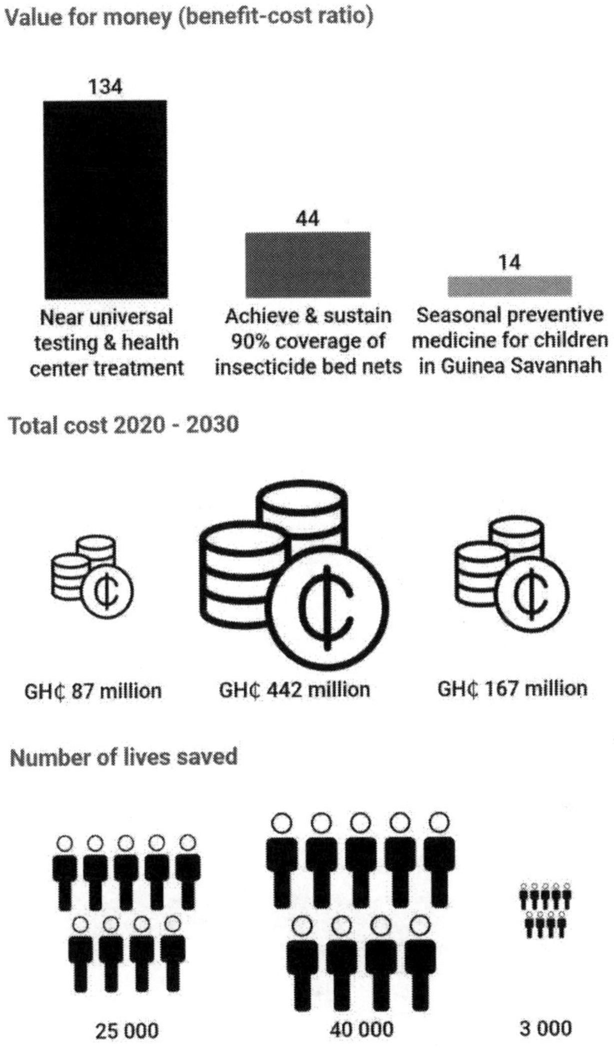

Source: Authors paper

Investments in Mental Health for Far-Reaching Benefits

Mental health problems are a major contributor to the disease burden across the world and in Ghana. They have a significant impact on individuals through increased disability and mortality, but they also generate substantial costs for Ghana and elsewhere in the form of lost productivity.

The costs of poor mental health have been conservatively estimated to account for between 3% and 4% of GDP in developing countries. Globally, the World Economic Forum and the Harvard School of Public Health have estimated the cost of mental illness at US$2.5 trillion every year, with a projected increase to US$6 trillion by 2030.

At an individual level, both patients and their caregivers experience economic costs due to mental health issues. Depression, for example, causes a 50% productivity loss for the patient and 24% for the caregiver. With schizophrenia, the loss in productivity is estimated at 70% for the patient and 30% for the caregiver.

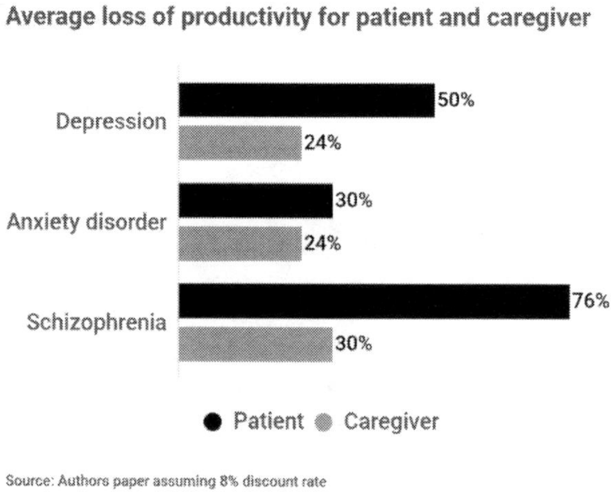

According to WHO estimates, approximately 13% of Ghana's population suffers from mental disorders, with schizophrenia, substance abuse, and mood disorders being the most common diagnoses. Mental disorders are one of the leading causes of years lived with disability in the country, and it has been predicted that there will be an increase in the number of young people entering the age of risk for onset of certain mental disorders.

Despite the prevalence and impact of these diseases, mental and neurological disorders often go undiagnosed and untreated, and investment in mental health is less than 1% of the health budget in many countries. In Ghana, the treatment gap for mental health disorders is estimated to be over 98%. Many people do not receive evidence-based care, which leads to chronicity, suffering and increased economic effects.

Encouraging better mental health through increased screening, early detection and intervention for severe mental disorders, particularly depression and schizophrenia, has the potential to reduce the high social and economic effects for both individuals and the society. However, with so many areas competing for the attention of policymakers, it is vital to know where scarce public resources can generate the biggest benefit not only in economic but also social and environmental terms.

On mental health, Justice Nonvignon and Samuel Agyei Agyemang from the School of Public Health at the University of Ghana, Caroline Reindorf Amissah from the Mental Health Authority in Accra, and Brad Wong from Copenhagen Consensus calculated the costs of screening approximately 980,000 people to detect cases of depression, anxiety and schizophrenia, as well as the cost of their treatment, including both medical and non-medical expenses. These costs were then compared to the benefits derived from correctly treating mental disorders.

With depression, the number of Ghanaians projected to be included in the programme after screening was estimated at 13,200. Treatment would last two years on average, but 30% of the cases would continue to receive some consultation and medication for life. The total cost of this intervention was estimated at approximately GH₵ 92 million for a period of 10 years, but the benefit for Ghana and especially its economy would be much larger. Through screening and treatment, 112 cases of self-harm and twelve suicides could be prevented each year.

The total benefits, including around GH₵ 560 million productivity loss avoided for patients and caregivers, were estimated at GH₵ 630 million, seven times more than the original investment.

For anxiety disorder, the number of Ghanaians projected to receive treatment was estimated at around 11,400, and about 30% would remain on antidepressants for life. The researchers estimated the total cost of this programme at approximately GH₵ 88 million, with benefits worth more than GH₵ 400 million. 97 cases of self-harm and nine suicides could be averted every year, as well as an estimated GH₵ 350 million in productivity loss for patients and caregivers. For every cedi spent on treating anxiety, nearly 5 cedi could be gained for society.

Schizophrenia patients would be enrolled in treatment for life, but the number of people the researchers estimated to receive treatment in Ghana is only 667, much lower than the number of patients with depression and anxiety. The projected cost for the schizophrenia programme was estimated at approximately GH₵ 28 million and the total benefit at GH₵ 44 million, including patient and caregiver productivity loss as well as five cases of self-harm and one suicide averted per year.

Overall, this research shows that screening and treatment for mental disorders in Ghana contributes to improved health and productivity in patients and caregivers, paving the path toward stronger economic participation and output for both within Ghana's economy.

Intervention	**BCR**	**Benefit (GH₵ Million)**	**Cost (GH₵ Million)**
Screening and treatment of depression for more than 13,200 people	6.9	634	92
Screening and treatment of anxiety disorders for almost 11,400 people	4.6	408	88
Screening and treatment of schizophrenia for 667 people	1.6	44	28

Total costs and benefits are discounted at 8%

Improving mental health

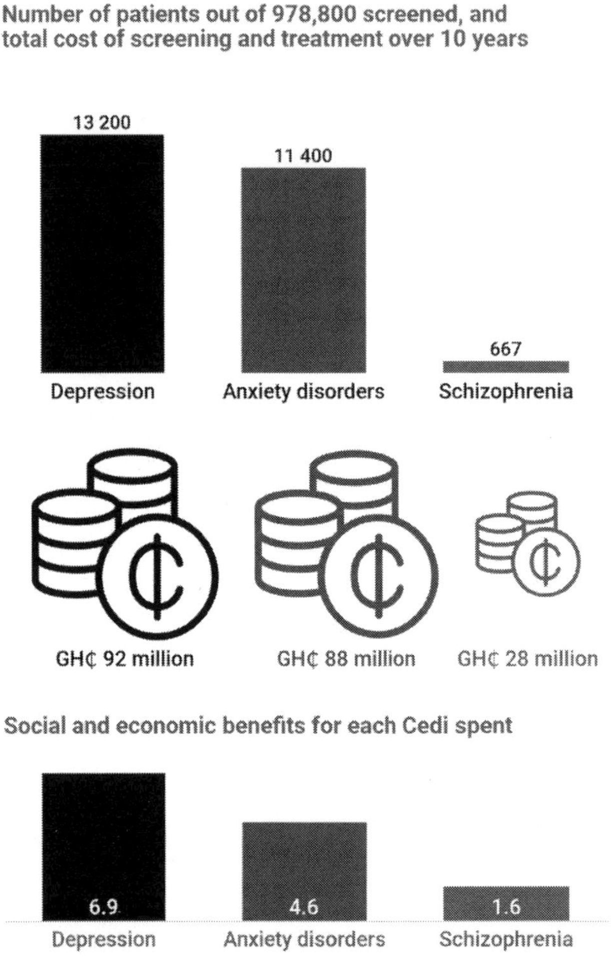

Source: Authors paper assuming 8% discount rate

Better Nutrition for a Prosperous Future

Healthy mothers and children are the foundation of a thriving nation, and the first 1,000 days of a child's life are the most critical for their future health. Nutrition in the prenatal stage and early childhood is fundamental to guaranteeing overall health and wellbeing, and it brings multiple benefits to the economy through a lowered rate of avoidable disease, and a boost in productivity throughout life.

Yet, Ghana faces many challenges, and nutrition is just one of them. There are many potentially incredible solutions to challenges from malaria to education, from better transportation to a more productive agriculture. Where should limited resources go first?

There is no doubt nutrition is an important part of the discussion. In a new research paper, Richmond Aryeetey from the University of Ghana, Paul Kwame Nkegbe and Haruna Issahaku from the University for Development Studies, and Brad Wong of Copenhagen Consensus have analysed the most cost-effective mechanisms to reduce childhood malnutrition and do the most good for every cedi spent. The economists took the best, published data to calculate the total benefits Ghana could achieve from adopting different nutrition policies to benefit the public.

Nutrition during pregnancy is crucial for a child's development. While 89% of pregnant women in Ghana already attend at least four antenatal appointments and 93% receive iron-folate supplementation, pre-eclampsia and anaemia in pregnant women are still prevalent and avoidable maternal deaths are unacceptably high.

Many of them could be prevented through additional supplementation with multiple micronutrients and calcium. Switching from one set of pills to another for all 850,000 pregnant women is relatively cheap at 202 million cedis annually, and could help avoid as many as 4,209 infant deaths, and 82 maternal deaths. Every cedi spent on the implementation of this proposal would produce 18 cedis of social benefit.

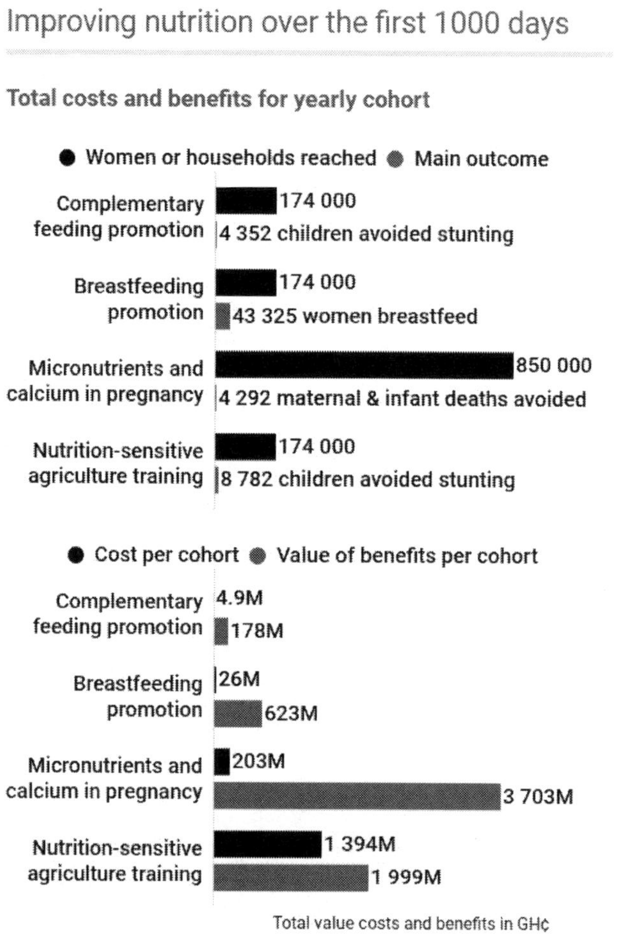

Source: Authors paper

Early adoption and continued exclusive breastfeeding during the first six months are extremely beneficial for a child's development and disease prevention. Increased breastfeeding counselling given to mothers in their prenatal and postnatal appointments, as well as improved training and protocols for healthcare professionals, would also have a great impact on health.

The costs would be shared at nearly equal parts by the women and the government: around 12 million GH₵ for the state to implement, and an hour per day of time and inconvenience cost for the women, valued at GH₵14 million.

Over the course of two years and with 174,000 mothers included in this initiative, 745 children's lives would be saved and approximately 160,000 cases of child illness avoided, which would create social benefits equal to approximately GH₵ 623 million. At the total cost of only GH₵26 million, every cedi spent would deliver social benefits worth 24 cedis.

Stunting, or being shorter than normal for a child's age, because of undernourishment, has been shown to hinder cognitive development and means that the child will do less well later in life.

If children get better nutrition their brain will develop better, they will learn more in school and become much more productive as adults. Imagine a policy that could help make Ghana's next generation even more productive. This is what ensuring that children have diets that are sufficiently diverse and provided at an optimal frequency up until five years of age is capable of achieving.

Child malnutrition could be reduced dramatically in Ghana through optimal complementary feeding promotion. The researchers found that one-on-one nutritional counselling given to 20 % of all new mothers would help reduce stunting in children by 9% and save 65 lives over the course of their first five years of life. Fewer cases of stunting would also mean a significant boost to the economy in long-term improved productivity.

At a cost of GH₵4.9 million, the benefits are significantly higher, at GH₵178 million. Each cedi spent on complementary feeding promotion will generate long-term social benefits worth 36 cedis.

The researchers also studied the effects of nutrition-sensitive agriculture. This initiative involves providing 174,000 households thirty to forty chickens, along with assistance and training in nutrition and gardening. The intervention would bring long-lasting benefits in health and increased income for the families involved but would be much more expensive to implement.

Costing 1,394 million cedi, the benefits would range from GH₵1,823 to GH₵2,174.

Improving nutrition over the first 1000 days

Value for money (benefit-cost ratio)

36x
Complementary feeding promotion reaching new mothers

24x
Breastfeeding promotion reaching new mothers

18x
Add multiple micronutrients and calcium to existing supplementation in pregnancy for 850,000 women

1.4x
Nutrition-sensitive agriculture training and 30-40 chickens to 174,000 households

The proposed policies give a great argument for Ghana to spend more of its scarce resources on nutrition to improve life. They certainly give the Minister of Health a great opportunity to showcase why the next budget should increase spending here.

Interventions	BCR	Benefit (GHȻ Million)	Cost (GHȻ Million)
MMN and CA supplementation in pregnancy	18	3,703	203
Breastfeeding promotion	24	623	26
Complementary feeding promotion	36	178	4.9
Nutrition-sensitive agriculture	1.3-1.6	1,823 to 2,174	1,394

Total costs and benefits are discounted at 8%

Focussed Actions to Reduce Poverty

Since 2000, Ghana's development has been a real success story. The country has witnessed sustained economic growth, with real GDP per capita increasing by 3.5% per year on average and extreme poverty levels falling by almost 80% according to the Ghana Statistical Service. However, in recent years poverty levels have barely changed nationally, and it appears to be worsening in certain parts of the country.

The rural savannah area contains 75% of the country's extreme poor, with 36% of the population living in extreme poverty, up from 27% in 2013. Remaining clusters of poverty will be harder and more expensive to eradicate, and public spending has to explore effective ways to make sure limited resources are used in the smartest ways possible.

Charles Adjasi from the Stellenbosch University in South Africa and Brad Wong from Copenhagen Consensus studied the effects of four well-known policy instruments designed to improve livelihoods: poverty graduation programs, cash transfers, microfinance, and social housing.

Poverty graduation, first developed in Bangladesh by the NGO BRAC, is a multi-faceted and intensive program that aims to permanently lift extremely poor households out of poverty. Households are given assets, typically livestock, and training that helps them use those assets to earn a living.

They are offered additional support throughout the two years of the program: cash, life coaching, health and banking services, and community integration. Research from across the world has shown that this initiative is successful in generating long-lasting boosts to income, assets and food security. For Ghana, the benefits would be worth GH₵ 17,600 to the household. However, the program is expensive, at GH₵ 9,600 per household. This still represents a return 1.8 times higher than the original investment.

Another initiative the researchers studied was Ghana's Livelihood Empowerment Against Poverty program (LEAP), that provides cash grants and health insurance to poor households. The intervention suggests increasing the stipend by 7% for 81,600 households living in regions with higher costs of living. This would require an additional GH₵ 13 million per year, or GH₵ 160 annually for eligible households.

Previous evaluations of LEAP have shown that households use the cash grants productively, and the researchers estimate that the benefits in increased consumption would be GH₵ 21 million per year equivalent to GH₵ 255 annually for every household. Every cedi spent on this initiative would produce social and economic good worth 1.6 cedis.

The researchers also considered expanding access to micro-finance. Close to half of Ghanaian households operate a non-farm household business, but access to credit to start and sustain these ventures is very limited.

Providing a microloan of GH₵ 3900, repayable over one year, would cost GH₵ 1100 in operation and financing expenses. The benefits are two-fold. The first is revenue for the microfinance institution which generates income equal to GH₵ 1200 from providing the credit service. The second is to the household.

Careful research shows that beneficiaries use microfinance to give them greater choice in how they generate their incomes.

This benefit of choice is worth GH₵ 500 according to the researchers. The total benefits of microfinance amount to GH₵ 1,700, with every cedi spent bringing a return of 1.6 cedis.

Approximately 65% of households in Ghana live in impoverished structures due to inadequate housing supply and infrastructure. That is why researchers also evaluated the benefits of increased social housing in urban areas. The initiative consists of generating two types of structures: two-bedroom semi-detached houses and high-rise apartments in urban areas. This intervention has the lowest return of the ones studied, costing an average of GH₵ 201,000 per beneficiary and bringing in a benefit of GH₵ 205,000. Still, that is not to say it would not greatly improve the lives of Ghana's urban poor.

Overall the researchers suggest that poverty graduation is likely to be the most effective use of public funds aimed at reducing poverty directly. Besides having the largest benefit-cost ratio, the program brings sustained benefits to the recipients throughout the course of their lives.

However, it is possible that other, *indirect* approaches to poverty might be more effective. This could focus on improved education or better health care, which for the same amount of cedis often can help much more. This conversation will continue over the coming weeks in The Daily Graphic to spur the discussion on future priorities for Ghana.

Intervention	**BCR**	**Benefit (GH₵ Million)**	**Cost (GH₵ Million)**
Poverty graduation	1.8	17,574	9,633
Increase cash transfers under LEAP	1.6	255	160
Microfinance	1.6	1,679	1,077
Social Housing	1.0	205,425	201,213

Note: Social housing intervention is an average of three types of housing. All figures assume an 8% discount rate.

Cost and benefits poverty interventions

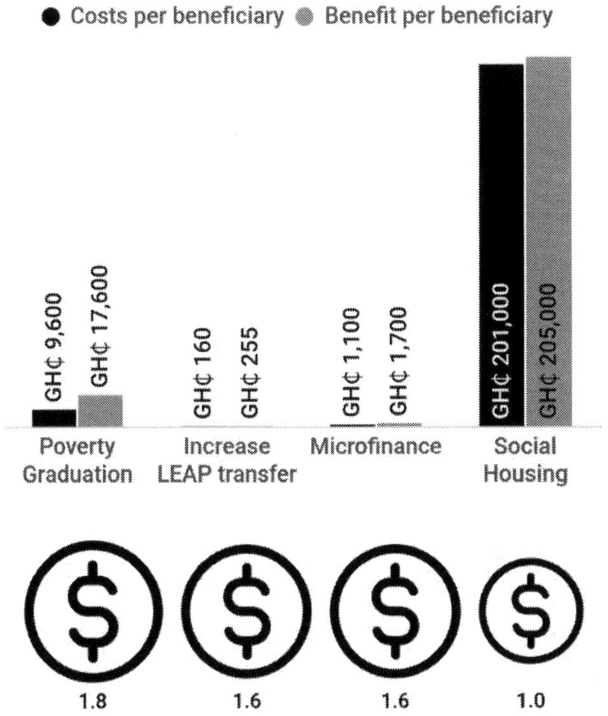

Value for money (benefit-cost ratio)

Source: Authors paper

Electricity for Health and Productivity

Expanding access to electricity can increase productivity and even improve health access, which makes it a vital component of development in rural areas. However, electricity access in rural Ghana was only 67% in 2018, and the northern parts of the country are in a notably worse situation compared to regions in the south.

In all three northern regions, national grid connection is less than 70%, due to most communities being located far from major voltage lines and having low population densities. These areas are also more difficult to access due to poor road infrastructure and difficult terrain.

To bridge the gap and provide electricity to Ghana's rural population, a combination of energy solutions is required. These initiatives could involve the use of both renewable and non-renewable sources of energy through grid extensions and local off-grid solutions, but decision-makers need to ensure the investment goes to the best possible policies.

Francis Kemausuor, Kwaku Amaning Adjei, John Bosco Dramani, and Prince Boakye Frimpong from the Kwame Nkrumah University of Science and Technology (KNUST), and Brad Wong of Copenhagen Consensus studied interventions to improve access to electricity in rural Ghana, using the well-representative Gushiegu Municipality of the Northern Region as a model.

The initiatives include the expansion of the national grid to less-remote communities, the use of solar and diesel micro-grids in small, remote communities, and finally, broadening the access to the national grid to all remaining, small communities.

Expanding the grid to the 79 less-remote communities would reach approximately 42,000 people or around 7,000 households in eight years. The researchers estimated the cost of connecting these communities at GHC 59 million, and the total cost, including electricity generation over 20 years, at around GHC 100 million. The result would be a 46% increase in gross household income through increased productivity.

Electrification would also incentivise health care workers to move to rural communities and increase the availability of services, leading to a 35% reduction in hospitalizations and one avoided death per every 4,500 individuals each year. In total, extending the national grid to less-remote communities would amount to benefits worth GHC 450 million in increased productivity and health, or 4.5 times the cost of the original investment.

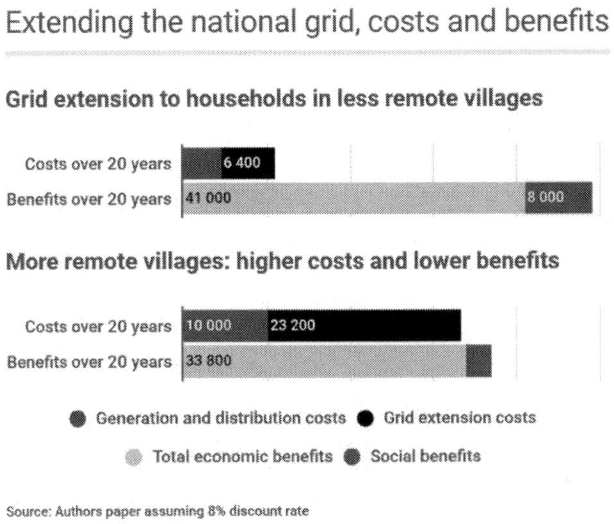

For small and remote communities, the researchers studied the option of a micro-grid, diesel or solar-powered, to generate and distribute electricity to a limited number of customers in isolation from national networks.

Diesel micro-grids, at approximately GHC 25,000 per household, are slightly more expensive than solar micro-grids, at GHC 20,000. However, they can also bring in higher benefits for each household, at GHC 45,000 over the GHC 34,000 of a solar grid connection. The researchers considered the total cost of 300 households being connected to diesel micro-grids by 2027, at GHC 7.6 million.

For solar-powered grids, the analysis included 1911 households, for a cost of GHC 38 million. The expected benefits in increased welfare and household income from the connection to a diesel micro-grid are 13.6 million, meaning every cedi invested in this initiative can yield a return of 1.8 cedis.

With solar-powered grids, the benefits are GHC 65 million, which takes the cost-benefit ratio to 1.7, slightly lower than diesel.

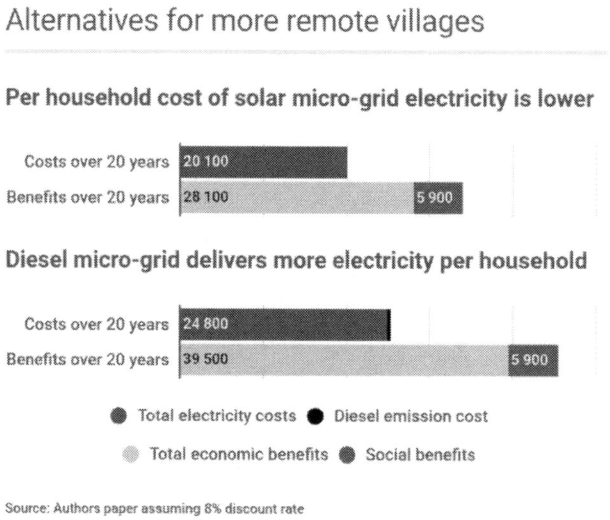

As an alternative to micro-grids, the researchers studied the possible expansion of the national grid to all remote communities of over 200 people in the municipality. The total costs were estimated at GHC 83 million for 2,493 households, and the benefits at GHC 92 million. The cost-benefit ratio of this intervention is 1.1, showing that for households in more remote communities, providing solar and diesel micro-grids yields slightly higher benefits than connecting them to the national grid.

If policymakers consider electrification as a must-have for Ghana's rural population, this cost-benefit analysis suggests that micro-grids are the best bet in remote areas. In the rural communities that are closer to the existing infrastructure and have a higher electricity demand, connecting them to the national grid is the most cost-effective solution.

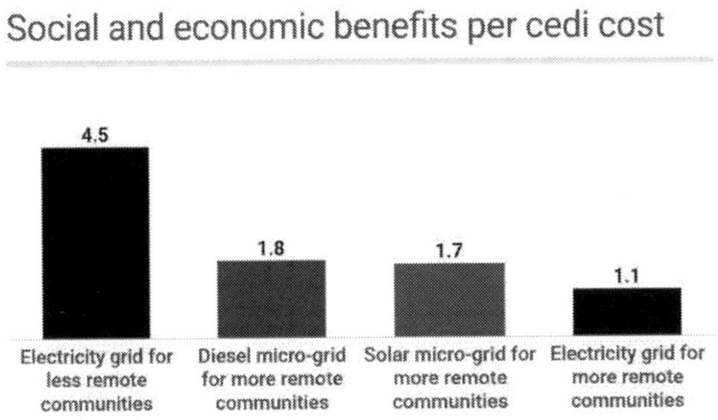

All these interventions pass the cost-benefit test and would undoubtedly improve the health and development of remote rural communities in the northern regions of Ghana.

Costs and Benefits per Household over 20 years

Interventions	BCR	Benefit (GH₵)	Cost (GH₵)
Electricity grid for less remote communities	4.5	48,948	10,940
Diesel micro-grid for more remote communities	1.8	45,344	25,358
Solar micro-grid for more remote communities	1.7	34,048	20,099
Electricity grid for more remote communities	1.1	36,761	33,250

Total Costs and Benefits over 20 years

Interventions	BCR	Benefit (GH₵ Million)	Cost (GH₵ Million)
Electricity grid for less remote communities	4.5	451.4	100.9
Diesel micro-grid for more remote communities	1.8	13.6	7.6
Solar micro-grid for more remote communities	1.7	65.6	38.4
Electricity grid for more remote communities	1.1	91.6	82.9

Total costs and benefits are discounted at 8%

Rural Sanitation for Cleaner and Healthier Communities

Clean and healthy communities require proper sanitation, but one in every three people in the world still lacks access to a dignified sanitation service. Ghana has also struggled to improve sanitation coverage, and the situation remains challenging, especially in rural communities where private latrines are scarce.

Throughout the entire UN Millennium Development Goals period, between 2000 and 2015, the percentage of rural households practising open defecation dropped by only one percentage point, to 31%. As of 2017, about 4 million people in rural Ghana still practised open defecation, and many others rely on facilities shared between more than one household.

The most significant consequence of poor sanitation is the high burden of diarrhoea and cholera. In 2017, Ghanaians suffered an estimated 41 million cases of diarrhoea and nearly 800 cases of cholera. Over 7,000 deaths were caused by diarrheal disease in the country, and more than 3,500 of them were children.

Sanitation is an urgent issue policymakers need to focus on in order to improve Ghanaians' overall health, but it's not the only one. While Ghana has seen impressive economic growth in the last two decades and the government has increased public spending to advance development, resources are always limited and decision-makers need to prioritise the smartest initiatives with the highest likelihood of success.

To improve sanitation in rural communities, a group of researchers for the Ghana Priorities project which aims to highlight the most cost-effective policy proposals for the country, studied the impact of the main community sanitation intervention used in rural Ghana, the Community-Led Total Sanitation (CLTS) model.

The CLTS initiative is a three-step process. First, communities are selected, information is collected to plan the intervention, and the implementers are trained. Second, the program aims to make community members aware of their current unsanitary conditions and practices and motivate them to engage with the program and construct latrines. In the final step, the implementers conduct follow-up visits to assess the success of the program.

The total costs of this intervention on its own were estimated at GH₵ 3.7 million for a nationally representative area of 100 villages and around 80,000 people. With this investment, the researchers predict a 15% average improvement in uptake rates for the latrines.

Households that build latrines see a 20% reduction in diarrheal disease, which translates into 31,000 cases of diarrhoea and 6 premature deaths avoided over a 10-year period. Additionally, beneficiaries would save 5 minutes a day from not having to find a place to open defecate – a staggering 80,000 hours over a 10-year period for these communities. The total benefits of the CLTS intervention were estimated at GH₵ 4.8 million, meaning every cedi spent on this initiative would produce 1.3 cedis of social benefit.

These figures mask the fact that not all villages respond to CLTS equally, with some greatly increasing the use of latrines, and others much less. This difference matters because health benefits are greater when a large proportion of the population in any community takes up improved sanitation.

The analysts assume that once latrine coverage reaches 75%, all households would see a reduction in disease rates of up to 35%. This way, even those that don't have a private latrine can eventually benefit from a successful implementation of the CLTS intervention.

One important reason households don't switch to improved sanitation is the cost of a latrine. Providing subsidies can help but because they are expensive, it is important that they are targeted to where they can be most effective. With this in mind, the researchers suggest a second intervention where the 40% poorest households in villages that respond well to CLTS are provided with a subsidy. They estimate this would increase the uptake rate of improved sanitation by 22%.

When the traditional CLTS intervention is coupled with the subsidy, the benefit in reduced disease and death also increases, to around 44,000 non-fatal diarrhoea cases and 9 premature deaths averted over the 10-year period. Across the region, more than 94,000 hours could also be saved by adopting the intervention, increasing the potential benefits in improved productivity for the communities.

The cost of this intervention, including the subsidy, is GH₵ 4.2 million, and the benefits reach nearly GH₵ 7 million, meaning they're now 1.7 times higher than the original investment.

The CLTS intervention passes a cost-benefit test both with and without a subsidy, showing that improved sanitation has an important effect on reducing disease and mortality. The initiative may also bring other non-health benefits, including a reduced risk of assault, increased dignity, and better privacy, all of which are especially relevant for women in particular.

Cleaner, healthier communities are also more productive, and the access to proper sanitation is key to unlocking their potential.

Interventions	**BCR**	**Benefit (GH₵ Million)**	**Cost (GH₵ Million)**
Community-Led Total Sanitation (CLTS) for 100 villages	1.3	4.8	3.7
CLTS for 100 villages with targeted subsidy for latrine construction	1.7	7.0	4.2

Total costs and benefits are discounted at 8%

Community-led total sanitation projects

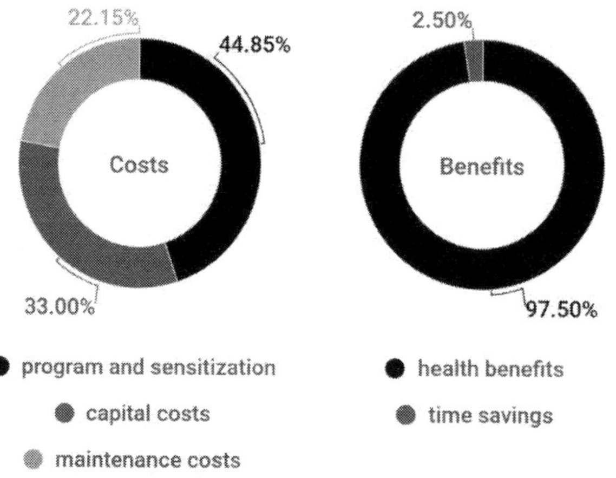

Total costs and benefits for an average village (GHC)

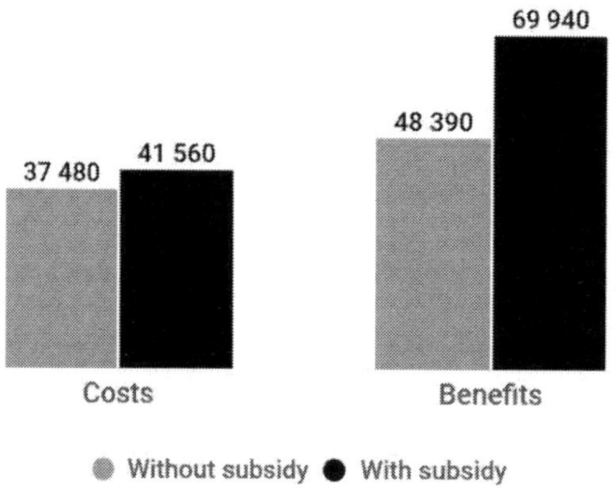

Higher social value-for-money from combining the CLTS investment with a targeted subsidy

Source: Authors paper assuming 8% discount rate, costs and benefits over 10 years

Prioritising Tuberculosis Treatment for Incredible Results

With news around the world focussing on the Corona crisis, it's easy to forget that one of the most common killers in Ghana and globally is a disease we already have a treatment for: tuberculosis (TB).

Approximately one-quarter of the world's population has been infected, although the majority don't ever develop active disease. Individuals with tuberculosis often remain undiagnosed and untreated, able to carry it on and infect others. According to WHO estimates, TB is responsible for 5% of total deaths every year in Ghana. It affects mostly the working age population, with 73% of cases between the ages of 15 and 44.

That's why TB is not only a health issue, it also impacts the overall productivity of the Ghanaian economy. Even with Ghana's economic progress and a notable increase in public spending in the past years, resources are limited and prioritising the right initiatives is a challenge.

To identify the best strategies to combat tuberculosis, Jamie Rudman and Rein Houben from the London School of Hygiene & Tropical Medicine, National Tuberculosis Control Programme manager Yaw Adusi Poku, and Saleema Razvi and Brad Wong from Copenhagen Consensus studied three important interventions to deal with the disease burden: active case finding in high-risk populations, improved speed and accuracy of diagnosis through implementation of molecular diagnostic tools, as well as education and counselling alongside Directly observed treatment short-course (DOTS) to make sure those receiving TB treatment adhere to the necessary treatment.

Altogether, they found these proposed initiatives would have a phenomenal impact on reducing the burden of long-term illness on households and the health care system.

Active case finding through community outreach and targeted screening and testing for tuberculosis uses chest X-rays and molecular testing with GeneXpert equipment for those that present with symptoms indicative of TB, specifically targeting high-risk populations including miners, refugees, and vulnerable urban populations. Test-positive individuals are registered and linked to a health facility to start treatment.

The intervention aims to reach 150,000 individuals in these high-risk groups, with the goal of identifying and giving treatment to 33% of total cases among these vulnerable populations by 2025. The total cost of additional screening and treatment is estimated at GH₵ 256 million by 2040. However, this initiative would have a significant impact on the burden of tuberculosis disease, with approximately 5,000 cases and 2,000 deaths avoided during the initial six years of scaleup of the programme.

In the longer term, the impact is even more impressive. By 2040, the intervention would help avoid 56,000 cases and 26,400 deaths with benefits for society worth GH₵ 10,000 million. Actively identifying tuberculosis cases this way equates to 38 cedis for every cedi invested in the intervention.

A sputum transportation system to link 1,000 health facilities to 126 existing molecular testing sites is another initiative that has already been implemented in Ghana with good results.

The researchers studied the effect of transporting samples from suspect cases in local health care facilities, to facilities with on-site GeneXpert testing capabilities, for faster and more accurate GeneXpert testing, hence reducing the need for individuals to travel to obtain TB test results, and increasing GeneXpert test coverage at the national level to 90 percent by 2025.

They estimated the total costs of this initiative at GH₵ 80 million over two decades. However, the scale-up of molecular testing would have a major impact the burden of disease, with around 65,000 tuberculosis cases avoided and 36,600 lives saved by 2040. The total social and economic benefits of the intervention would amount to more than GH₵ 13,000 million, yielding a return of 166 cedis for every cedi spent.

Even with the improved diagnosis methods, individuals diagnosed with TB are often lost to follow-up once enrolled on DOTS. Therefore, the researchers also assessed the impact of education and counselling of tuberculosis to increase treatment adherence and overall completion and success.

This intervention was estimated to lead to an additional 16% increase in the proportion completing treatment successfully, with 31,000 TB cases and 13,200 deaths avoided. The costs of training course development, and nurse training time, as well as costs incurrent by individuals with TB and their households are estimated at GH₵ 26 million in total, but the total benefits are worth almost GH₵ 5 billion.

Every cedi spent on this initiative yields benefits worth 190 cedi, making this the most cost-effective solution on the wide spectrum of public health policies.

Tuberculosis, if treated in a timely fashion, has a high cure rate. Despite the moderate cost of screening and treatment, it is still the number one infectious killer in the world and one of the most common ailments in Ghana. The benefit-cost ratios for tackling TB are some of the largest in the entire Ghana Priorities project, which shows the importance and the potentials of addressing this disease as a priority.

Accurately identifying individuals with TB and making sure they follow the treatment has an incredible potential for saving lives, and the government could make a large impact on Ghanaians' lives with a holistic approach that includes all three of these potentially highly efficient policies.

Saving lives from tuberculosis until 2040

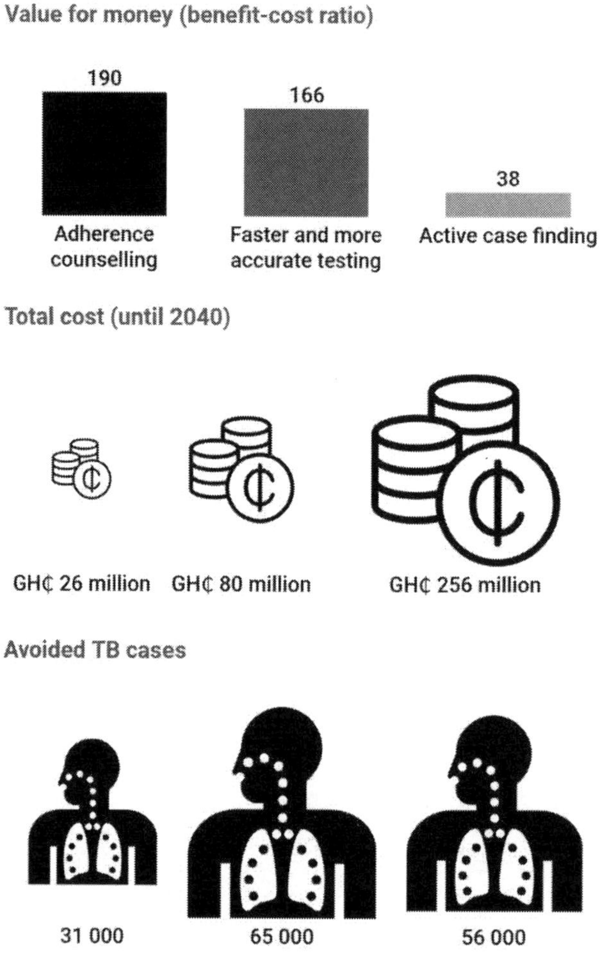

Source: Authors paper

Costs and benefits over 22 years

Interventions	BCR	Benefit (GHC Million)	Cost (GHC Million)
Sputum transportation system	166	13,255	80
Adherence counselling	190	4,839	26
Active case finding	38	9,654	38

Total costs and benefits are discounted at 8%

TRANSFORMED TRANSPORTATION TO BOOST GROWTH

Ghana has been experiencing steady economic development, but GDP growth has not been supported with enough infrastructure to boost welfare sustainably in the long term. One of the sectors requiring urgent improvement is transport.

The road network comprises over 78,000 kilometres, but only 49% of it is maintained or rehabilitated. Up to 60% of the 1300-kilometre rail network is not used regularly due to lack of maintenance.

This absence of necessary infrastructure limits commerce and exports, and slows down Ghana's economic growth prospects and even tourism, given that many of the major attractions are located in rural areas and difficult to reach due to the poor overall state of the roads.

Accra's rapid demographic growth also creates transportation issues through an increased number of vehicles and congestion. As the city spreads, people experience longer commutes, which creates time costs and has an adverse impact on the environment. But with so many important challenges, how can decision-makers choose the right initiatives to generate the highest benefit for every cedi spent?

To answer this, Bahman Kashi and Sarah Carello from Limestone Analytics, Michael Graham from the University of Stellenbosch Business School in South Africa, and Brad Wong of Copenhagen Consensus studied infrastructure interventions to target the country's rural areas as well as Accra's growing traffic congestion.

The researchers studied the construction of 1888 km of roads that link rural areas, especially agricultural areas and tourist attractions, to principal centres in the country. This initiative would have a cost of approximately GH₵ 5.3 billion, but the benefit from a reduction in travel time, carbon emissions, transportation cost and post-harvest losses avoided over 30 years was estimated at GH₵ 6.5 billion. For every cedi spent, this intervention would yield a return of 1.2 cedis.

Railway transport is a viable and affordable alternative to roads, especially for cargo and freights. However, Ghana's railway sector is in a poor state of maintenance, and today only accounts for 3% of freight traffic. A modern railway system would improve Ghana's international competitiveness and market access, stimulate productivity and boost economic growth and social welfare.

The researchers studied an intervention to rehabilitate 670 km of existing tracks and expand rail networks to the northern region of Ghana by constructing new tracks, with a total length of 3340 km. The cost of this project was estimated at GH₵ 73 million per kilometre.

The benefits in time savings, revenue from increased passenger traffic, the lower cost of transport, as well as reduced carbon emissions, accidents and post-harvest losses for the agricultural sector, add up to an estimated GH₵ 109 million per kilometre, meaning every cedi spent would yield a return of 1.5 times higher than the original investment.

The researchers also considered a transportation intervention to develop the Volta Lake into a major transportation artery and improve access to the rural northern regions and landlocked neighbouring countries by building modern ferry ports in Mpakadan, Buipe and Debre, and providing upgraded ferries in collaboration with the private sector.

The improved transport system would improve access to ferry transport for communities living in the surrounding area, which is currently served by an informal service of boats and roads in poor condition.

The costs of this intervention amount to approximately GH₵ 4.7 billion, while the benefits in cost savings, reduced carbon emissions and improved safety for passengers reach nearly GH₵ 5.8 billion, for a benefit-cost ratio of 1.2.

For Accra's growing traffic congestion problem, the researchers studied the option of investing in infrastructure for a Bus Rapid Transport (BRT) system that would include the construction of a separate bus lane to reduce travel times and make the bus a more attractive choice for passengers.

The costs associated with this project amount to nearly GH₵ 1.2 billion in total. However, the benefits in time savings from reduced congestion and carbon emissions and increased safety for all road users amount to nearly GH₵ 1.8 billion, generating 1.5 times the benefit for every cedi spent.

Extensive infrastructure projects are costly, but these initiatives have the potential to transform Ghana's transportation system, protect the environment, boost competitiveness and stimulate the country's growth prospects.

By linking rural areas to cities via road, rail and ferry and easing Accra's traffic congestion to save costs and time, decision-makers can bring both short-term comfort and long-lasting change for the people.

Summary Table

Interventions	BCR	Benefit (GH₵)	Cost (GH₵)
Linking agricultural producing areas and tourist attractions to district capitals	1.2	6.5 billion	5.3 billion
Rehabilitating 668 km of rail and constructing 3340 km of new rail	1.5	109 million per kilometre	73 million per kilometre
Volta River Transport System	1.2	5.8 billion	4.7 billion
Bus Rapid Transport System for Accra	1.5	1.8 billion	1.2 billion

Total costs and benefits are discounted at 8%

Cost-Effective Strategies to Reduce Flooding

Over the past decades, the Accra Metropolitan Area has witnessed major development, but this growth has given rise to risks of its own. Rapid urbanization has caused an unplanned expansion of built-up areas like roads, parking lots and other structures with impervious surfaces, which has led to perennial flooding.

Inadequacies of drainage systems and poor solid waste management add to this threat that is only bound to intensify in the future as climate change poses further challenges on cities and nations. Accra urgently needs a comprehensive flood risk mitigation strategy that includes environmental sanitation, drainage facilities and improved waste management.

Inclusive, long-term urban development planning is vital to channel water safely and prevent flooding damage for thousands of inhabitants of Accra.

To target the problem of flooding in Accra, Prof. Martin Oteng-Ababio and Prof. Austin Ablo from the University of Ghana and Dr. Brad Wong of Copenhagen Consensus studied three interventions: the construction of retention ponds for stormwater runoff, widening storm drains, and a community-led solid waste management project.

Increased flooding in Accra is partly a result of the rapid expansion of sealed-off surfaces along the Akuapim hills that reduce the absorption of water. The study proposes the construction of two retention ponds with additional storage capacity in the middle and upstream of the Odaw basin to help temporarily store water from peak flood events and gradually release it.

This will tremendously improve the safety and living conditions of the low-income communities suffering from perennial flooding downstream. The researchers calculated the total social costs for the ponds until the year 2050 at GH₵ 222 million, with part of the cost from building and monitoring, and most of the cost due to the smell and increased risk of mosquito borne illnesses from the ponds. However, the total benefits from reduced flood damage and less business and transport interruption reach GH₵ 285 million.

Every cedi invested on building retention ponds would yield a benefit of 1.3 cedis.

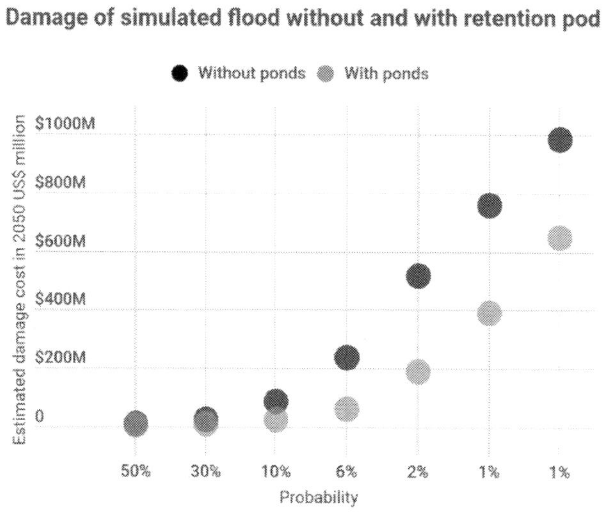

Source: World Bank (2019)

Properly functioning drainage systems are crucial to flood prevention, which is why the researchers also studied the construction of improved concrete storm drains with increased capacity, placed at bottleneck locations in the western part of the Akuapim Hills.

The construction costs for the storm drains were estimated at GH₵ 124 million and the total costs of the intervention, including maintenance until the year 2050, would reach GH₵ 216 million. This intervention would potentially lead to a 12% reduction of flood damages, as well as roughly 25,000 cases of diarrhoea and two deaths avoided every year in the communities surrounding the drains.

Overall, the benefits of improved drains are GHC 379 million, meaning each cedi produces social and economic good worth 1.8 cedis.

Storm drain widening costs and benefits over 40 years

Source: Researchers' calculation.

The researchers finally studied an initiative to minimise the mismanagement of solid waste that blocks drains and increases flood damage through participatory processes and community-based waste management.

The proposed model uses members of the community to collect household waste on specially designed tricycles, consolidating them at collection points for transportation to landfills or local composting stations. The use of community members is critical to ensure proper sorting and disposal.

Areas of high waste generation like slums and markets are identified and separated into groups of approximately 50,000 people or 12,500 households, and each camp is contracted out to a service provider who undertakes waste collection and management including sweeping, clearing of gutters and fumigation. The costs of the intervention include skips and bins for each camp and ongoing operational costs, amounting to around GHC 6.1 million per camp over a five-year period.

There are several benefits to this intervention, including the removal of waste, a generally cleaner environment within the community, improved health and reduced flooding. These benefits were estimated to be equivalent to GH₵ 6.4 million per camp. Every cedi spent on this initiative would thus yield a benefit of 1.1 cedis.

Photo from researchers' field work.

As economic growth increases in the metropolitan area, so does the risk of flooding, exacerbated by urbanization and the effects of climate change. These interventions offer policymakers a comprehensive strategy to tackle the existing hazards and prevent even greater risks in the future.

Interventions	BCR	Benefit (GH₵ Millions)	Cost (GH₵ Millions)
Storm Drain Widening for Accra	1.8	379	216
Two retention ponds for Accra	1.3	285	222
Community Solid Waste Management for 50,000 people	1.1	6.4	6.1

Total costs and benefits are discounted at 8%

Solutions for reduction of urban flooding

Value for money (benefit-cost ratio)

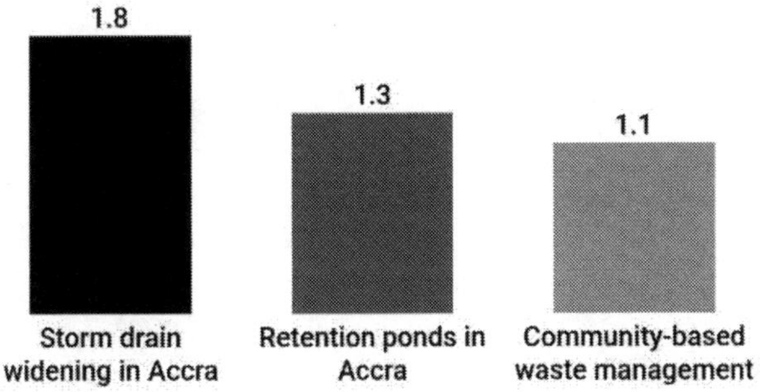

Source: Researchers' calculation.

BETTER HEALTH THROUGH IMPROVED URBAN SANITATION

Around 2.5 billion people in the world lack access to dignified sanitation services. In Ghana, coverage is abysmally low. Only 22% of the urban population have improved, non-shared facilities with shared toilets the most common service option in cities, accounting for over 60% of coverage.

With rapid urbanization further complicating the issue, sanitation is a serious challenge for the country. Programs to improve the situation have been implemented, but no systematic scale-up has so far been projected to boost urban sanitation across the country.

Studies have confirmed strong links between sanitation and health. Poor sanitation contributes to several tropical diseases, undernutrition and diarrhoea, a major public health threat and a leading cause of disease and mortality among children under five years.

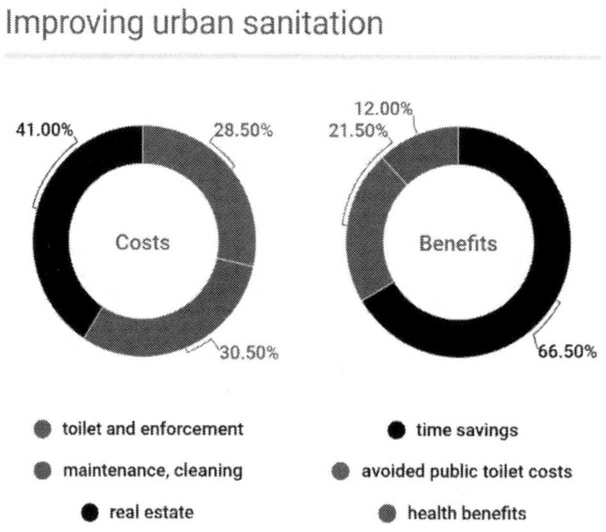

Source: Authors paper assuming 8% discount rate, costs and benefits over 20 years

It also causes a loss of productivity due to time lost for work or spent taking care of loved ones, and queuing for public or compound toilets. Access to improved sanitation services is a key target in the UN Sustainable Development Goals, and low coverage, especially in urban settings, is considered a threat to achieving almost all other goals.

To find effective solutions to Ghana's urban sanitation problem, Bismark Dwumfour-Asare from the University of Education in Winneba, independent consultant Bjorn Larsen, and Brad Wong from Copenhagen Consensus studied interventions that provide toilet subsidies for urban households.

They focussed on both the impact of a subsidy alone and a subsidy with additional support to metropolitan, municipal and district assemblies for better enforcement of sanitation by-laws.

Both interventions target urban households and compounds practicing open defecation, using public toilets or sharing a toilet, with the interim goal of reaching a situation where no more than three households would share improved sanitation facilities. The subsidy aimed at lessening the cost burden would be of approximately GH₵ 4000, equivalent to the cost of a bio-digester toilet. Extra enforcement would add an incentive for households and landlords to meet their obligation.

While enforcement makes the intervention more expensive, it also improves compliance and is more likely to have a larger effect on Ghana's urban sanitation situation. The cost of the subsidy with improved enforcement over a 20-year period was estimated by the researchers at GH₵ 16 billion assuming 75% of households targeted actually build a toilet.

Toilet subsidy with improved by-law enforcement

Source: Authors paper assuming 8% discount rate, costs and benefits over 20 years

The government would only pay for about a quarter of this cost — about GH₵ 4 billion — whereas the vast majority of cost falls on households and landlords. This includes toilet cleaning and maintenance costs, and lost rental space worth GH₵ 5 billion and GH₵ 7 billion respectively. However, the value of benefits from the intervention over the 20-year period is much higher, estimated at GH₵ 69 billion. 416 lives could be saved and two million cases of disease avoided per year.

But the largest benefits would come from increased productivity and cost savings from no longer having to use public toilets. Every cedi spent on this initiative would yield a benefit worth a little over 4 cedis.

The researchers also studied providing only a subsidy equivalent to 100% of the toilet cost, without emphasis on enforcement of sanitation bylaws. Existing enforcement regimes would continue without the intervention directly seeking any improvement, which means the uptake rate would be significantly lower. The cost was estimated at approximately GH₵ 2 billion in total, shared between the government, landlords and households, and the benefit at over GH₵ 11 billion.

This intervention would generate social and economic benefits more than 5 times higher than the original investment, but at an average uptake rate of only 10% would do little to help resolve Ghana's critical urban sanitation problem.

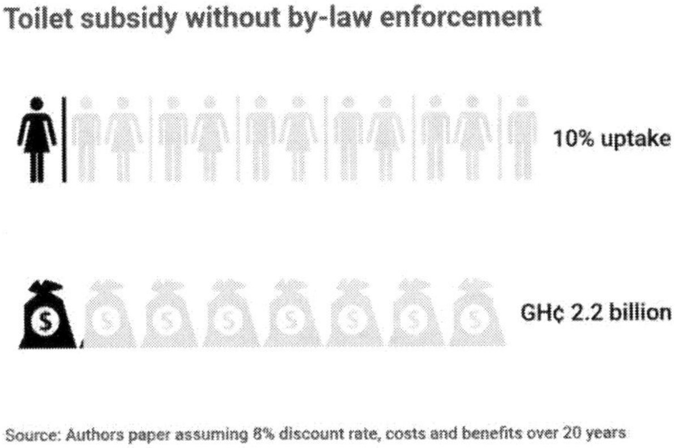

High population densities and demand for rental room destined for living instead of toilets contribute to non-shared sanitation rates being so low in Ghanaian cities. However, these interventions could increase rental revenues for landlords, given that tenants would likely be willing to pay more for units with improved sanitation.

Overall, this study provides policymakers with data-backed options to improve urban sanitation, moving Ghana closer to achieving its development goals.

Interventions	BCR	Benefit (GH₵ Millions)	Cost (GH₵ Millions)
Toilet subsidy provision (10% uptake)	5.2	11,384	2,190
Toilet subsidy provision with improved enforcement of sanitation by-laws (75% uptake)	4.2	69,061	16,344

Total costs and benefits are discounted at 8%

Skilled Youths for Improved Employment

A third of Ghana's population is between the ages of 15 and 34, but the country struggles to offer employment for its youth. Job creation has not kept up the pace with the country's strong GDP growth, and among young people unemployment has increased from 10% in 2008 to 14% in 2018, far exceeding the rate for adults.

Ghana also has lower levels of labour productivity than other African countries with a similar economic standing, partly because of inadequate training, and industries experience a lack of employable workers with the relevant skills for their tasks.

Productivity and job creation are critical issues that require urgent attention, and the government has initiated policies over the last decade to help the country take advantage of its youthful population.

To improve employment generation for Ghana's youths, Dr. Charles Ackah and Dr. Kwadwo Opoku from the University of Ghana and Dr. Brad Wong of Copenhagen Consensus studied three interventions used widely around the world to improve skill development and bridge the gap between labour market needs and young job-seekers: vocational training, apprenticeships, and start-up incubators.

Vocational education refers to the study of technologies and sciences, and the acquisition of practical skills and knowledge necessary for various occupations. Three years of technical education cost around GH₵ 34,000 per person, divided between direct costs for the government and the time and income forgone for the student.

The researchers project vocational training can lead to a significant productivity increase, reflected in a wage increase of 47%, or GH₵ 44,000 over the person's lifetime. Every cedi spent would generate 1.30 cedis of social good when compared to a scenario where instead the student goes into the workforce after basic education. If vocational education is compared to a student who instead goes on to senior high school the benefit is even higher, at 2.4 times the original investment.

This is because the extra years spent in school do not lead to much of a boost in the student's future wages, making the vocational education path relatively more attractive.

To increase the number of students enrolling in vocational education, the government should build more technical institutes, create awareness and help ensure job opportunities in private-public partnership companies to absorb graduates.

Clothing and other important items needed for learning may also serve as barriers for poor households to enrol their children in secondary schools, so removing these costs for students of vocational and technical training institutes may also improve levels of enrolment.

Estimated earnings profiles

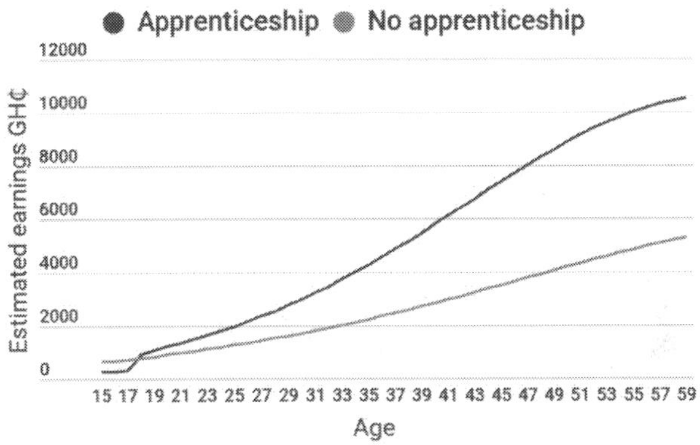

Source: Authors' computations from Gender and Enterprise Development Survey data

Apprenticeship is the main institution through which people with junior high school or lower levels of education are provided with training in Ghana. This practice has traditionally been informal but highly extended in many sectors, from trades and crafts to agriculture and business. Apprenticeships are beneficial to firms' revenues and profits and more flexible than traditional vocational training. Students also gain more relevant skills, because they do hands-on work and learn by observation.

The researchers estimate the cost of formal apprenticeship training at GHC 6,000 per person, and a lifetime wage increase for each participant is 65% compared to those with no apprenticeship training. The total benefits were estimated at nearly GHC 15,000, including additional benefits to the firm from hiring the apprentice.

Every cedi spent on apprenticeships would thus generate a return worth 2.40 cedis.

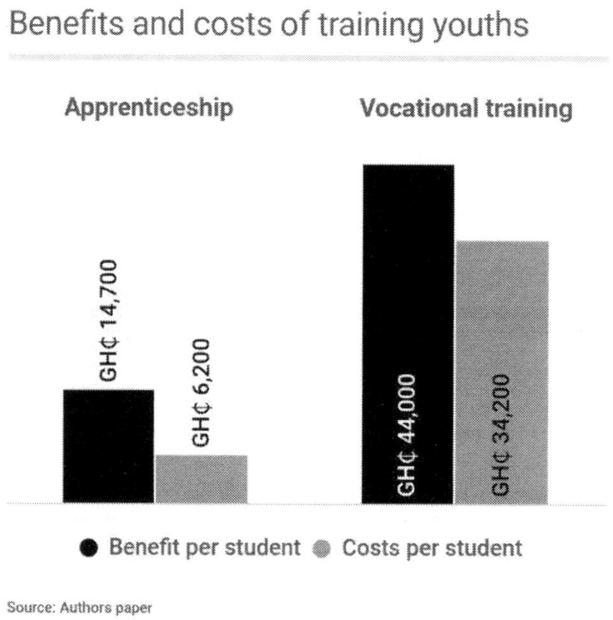

The possibility of helping small and medium enterprises through start-up incubators was also studied, but a lack of reliable data impedes the development of a cost-benefit analysis. However, small and medium companies are a source of massive employment creation in economies around the world, and boosting their growth can be useful for helping private sector development.

Measures to increase skill levels among Ghana's youths can help improve both employment rates and economic growth. Skilled workers may also boost the productivity of the economy and improve wages, so the overall impact of the interventions could be even higher than projected in this study.

Among the educational interventions studied in the Ghana Priorities project, quality primary education has a higher impact on increasing productivity in the long term than initiatives focusing on senior high school or job training. Still, the challenge of unemployed and unskilled youths is urgent and pressing, and beneficiaries of early childhood interventions will only hit the workforce in 10-15 years. Vocational training and apprenticeships can help improve this situation.

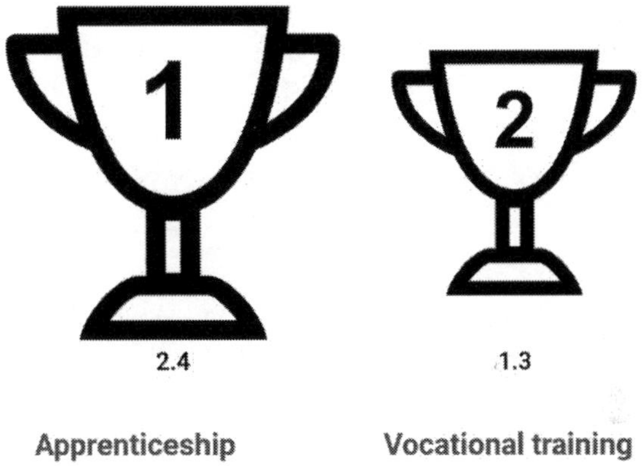

Interventions	BCR	Benefit (GH₵ per individual)	Cost (GH₵ per individual)
Vocational training	1.3	44,000	34,200
Apprenticeship	2.4	14,700	6,200

Total costs and benefits are discounted at 8%

Boosting Ghana's Industry for Sustained Growth

Ghana's economic growth has been rapid since the start of the new millennium, reaching 14% in 2011, but economic performance has been relatively lower since then, particularly from 2013-2016. Important factors for the slowing of development are the huge infrastructural deficit and the limited fiscal space, but Ghana has potential for improvement thanks to its large natural resource deposits.

The country has historically relied on the extraction of these abundant resources for economic and social development, and global business attention has focused on several sectors, including oil and gas, timber, cocoa, gold, diamond, bauxite, aluminium, and manganese.

However, infrastructural deficits impose restrictions on the growth drivers of the economy and undermine efforts for structural transformation. According to the National Development Planning Commission (NDPC), Ghana needs an annual infrastructural investment of GH₵ 9 billion for the next ten years, but growing public debt and its associated financing costs currently absorb over 45% of non-oil tax revenue.

To improve Ghana's industrial sector, Prof. Godfred A. Bopkin from the University of Ghana and Dr. Brad Wong from Copenhagen Consensus studied the costs and benefits of setting up an integrated bauxite authority to facilitate mining, processing, and transforming bauxite into alumina and aluminium.

According to the government, an integrated aluminium industry could potentially create 35,000 new jobs directly and indirectly, and contribute close to GH₵ 60 billion in economic output annually, equivalent to roughly 15% of the country's GDP.

The aluminium value chain consists of three main levels, from mining bauxite, which is the primary mineral for aluminium production, to refining it into alumina, and finally smelting it in the existing VALCO smelter to produce aluminium for industrial consumption.

The country already has several elements that would allow it to maintain the entire value chain in the country: an estimated bauxite reserve of about 900 million metric tonnes, large natural gas reserves to power its industries, an existing smelter, expanded ports, and significant quantities of industrial salt.

Each of the processes in the value chain involves a series of costs and benefits, and the researchers examined all the combinations of variables to reach an estimate of the potential impact of this intervention. The study included various controllable and uncontrollable factors, such as production volumes and costs of raw materials, resulting in 27 different scenarios for the cost of mining bauxite, producing alumina and, finally, aluminium.

These scenarios yielded annual total costs between GH₵ 5.9 billion and GH₵ 18.5 billion, and a median cost of all 27 scenarios for the entire value chain of GH₵ 12.4 billion per year.

Benefits and costs for different production volumes

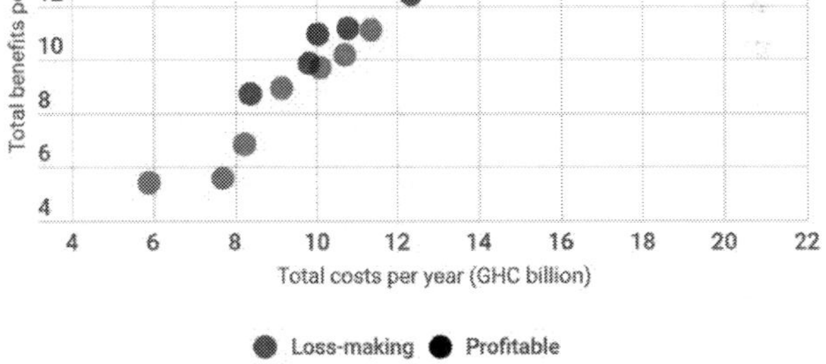

Source: Authors paper

The analysis of benefits also yielded 27 different scenarios based on similar controllable and uncontrollable factors, from production volume to the market price of the commodity. The total potential benefits fluctuate between GH₵ 5.4 billion and GH₵ 21 billion, with a median value of GH₵ 13.2 billion. Given the various cost estimates, the net benefit for the entire value chain ranges between a loss of GH₵ 2.1 billion and a gain of GH₵ 3.2 billion.

Overall, the processing of 5-20 million tonnes of bauxite into alumina and aluminium could provide an average net benefit of GH₵ 810 million every year, or roughly 0.24% of Ghana's GDP.

Analysis of an Integrated Alumina Industry

Best case scenario 1% of GDP in profit

- low power costs and high prices for aluminium, high production
- lower alumina production cost and 5% discount rate on investment
- bauxite is mainly produced for Ghanaian use

Worst case scenario loss of 0.6% of GDP

- high power costs and low aluminium prices, low production
- high alumina production cost and 14% discount rate on investment
- bauxite is sold at the lowest price but produced under the maximum operating cost

Average case 0.24% of GDP in profit

- average power costs and average aluminum prices
- average alumina production cost and 8% discount rate on investment
- bauxite is sold at the average price, at an average production cost

More benefits not included

social benefits from direct and indirect employment

Additional costs not included

destruction to the local economy that hinged on the forest, loss of community livelihoods and other living creatures, water bodies

Source: Authors paper

While these values are characterized by large fluctuations, the average benefit cost-ratio of 1.07 suggests that investing in this intervention is likely to be economically viable by producing benefits slightly higher than the original investment.

There are other expected positive effects that were not included in the study, such as technological transfers and direct and indirect employment that will be greater if alumina and aluminium are produced in the country instead of exporting raw bauxite. However, this analysis does not include the costs associated with the destruction of the natural environment required to mine bauxite.

Still, keeping the entire value chain from bauxite mining to aluminium production in Ghana will help develop the industry, create jobs and boost overall growth even in the long term.

This study shows that reforms and broad-based infrastructure support can provide more opportunities for growth and scale up efficiency across the board.

Total costs and benefits median of all scenarios

Intervention	BCR	Benefits	Costs
Mining, processing, and transformation of bauxite into alumina and aluminium	1.07	GH₵ 13.23 billion per year	GH₵ 12.36 billion per year

Ghana Priorities
Eminent Panel Findings

The Ghana Priorities Eminent Panel comprises:

- Mr Kenneth Ofori-Atta
- Prof. George Gyan-Baffour
- Prof. Sister Euginia Amporfu
- Prof. Kwesi Botchwey
- Prof. Augustin Fosu
- Prof. Ernest Aryeetey
- Prof. Finn E. Kydland

The Eminent Panel sought to address the research proposals with a view to answering the question: *On which initiatives should additional resources be spent first?*

The Eminent Panel intends these findings to be informative not just to the Government of Ghana, but also to others, including NGOs and charitable organizations.

The panel examined the proposals in detail. Each proposal was discussed with its principal author. The panel was informed by Sector Expert Commentaries, and by Panel members' own critical appraisals and discussions on assumptions and methodology.

In ordering the proposals, the Eminent Panel was guided predominantly by consideration of social, economic and environmental costs and benefits.

The Eminent Panel acknowledged the difficulties that cost-benefit analysis must overcome, both in principle and as a practical matter, but agreed that the cost-benefit approach was a very important organizing method.

Each Eminent Panel member assigned his own ranking to proposals. The Eminent Panel's ranking was calculated by taking the median of individual rankings.

The Eminent Panel jointly endorses the median ordering as representing their agreed view.

Ranking of Proposals

The Eminent Panel considers and prioritizes specific proposals to respond to challenges. This is different from ranking the challenges themselves. A low ranking of a proposal does not mean that the problem it addresses should be considered unimportant.

In ordering the proposals, the Eminent Panel was guided predominantly by consideration of social, economic and environmental costs and benefits. The Eminent Panel acknowledged the difficulties that cost-benefit analysis must overcome, both in principle and as a practical matter, but agreed that the cost-benefit approach was a very important organizing method.

The Ranking was calculated by taking the median of each Eminent Panel member's individual rankings. The Eminent Panel jointly endorses the median ordering as representing their agreed view. In due course, the Eminent Panel's individual commentaries shall be published in book form.

In setting priorities, the Eminent Panel has taken into account the strengths and weaknesses of the specific cost-benefit appraisals under review, and has given weight both to the institutional preconditions for success and to the demands of ethical or humanitarian importance.

Based on the costs and benefits of the solutions and their own assessment, the panel ranked the proposals, in descending order of desirability, as follows

Rank	Proposal	BCR
1	Digitized property and business fees	9
2	Universal malaria testing and health facility treatment	133
3	Strengthen community health system (GEHIP)	38
4	Land titling program	91
5	TB patient education for adherence	190
6	Logistics for faster and more accurate TB testing	166

7	Active TB case finding in high risk groups	38
8	Ambulance maintenance in rural areas	21
9	Preventive malaria medicine for children in Guinea Savannah	14
10	Complementary feeding promotion	36
11	Breastfeeding promotion	24
12	Management training for medium sized firms	18
12	Micronutrients and calcium in pregnancy	10
14	Incentive schemes for health workers in remote areas	21
15	Doubled R&D spending	28
15	Health worker home visits for pregnant and newborn	1.5
17	Build warehouses to reduce post-harvest losses	1.8
17	Vocational education	1.3
19	Revamp irrigation schemes	1.5
20	Increase mechanization through tractor services	2.8
21	Extend fertilizer subsidies	4.4
22	Hybrid maize seed subsidies	3.6
23	OPV maize seed subsidies	4.2
23	Enforcement by-laws and latrine subsidies in urban areas	2.3
25	Organize all 1-3 graders according to learning level	8
25	Depression screening and treatment	7
27	Apprenticeships	2.4
28	Community dialogues on schooling & early marriage	3.8
29	Support weaker 1-3 graders with teaching assistants	6
30	Raise and sustain coverage of malaria bed nets	44
31	Monitoring devices on trawl ships	21
32	Expand school feeding	4.8
33	Management consultants for large manufacturers	6
34	Emergency obstetric and neonatal care (EmONC)	6
34	Electricity grid for less remote communities	4.5
36	Capital grants for micro enterprises	34
36	Family planning for married women	7
36	Biogas to energy plants	4.7
39	Anxiety disorders screening and treatment	4.6
40	Replacement of illegal gears	5
41	Improved cookstoves promotion to reduce urban air pollution	8
42	Subsidize urban toilet constructions	12
42	Credit reference bureau	5

42	Expanded rural LPG distribution for cooking	2.1
45	Conditional asset transfer for girls enrolled in school	2.7
46	Solar microgrids for more remote communities	1.5
46	Revamp rail network for rural transport	1.7
48	Feeder roads for rural transport	1.2
49	Family planning for unmarried women	29
50	Electricity grid for more remote communities	1.1
51	Poverty graduation	1.8
52	Comprehensive faecal sludge treatment plants	5
52	Sludge to energy plants	3.3
52	Mass screening and treatment of hypertension	2.9
55	Compulsory SRH education for high school boys and girls	9
55	Improved cookstoves promotion to reduce rural air pollution	4.4
55	Fishing Licences and Aquaculture	2.2
55	Stabilization ponds for remote areas	1.2
59	Subsidize private senior high schools to increase seats	1.5
60	Eliminate NHIS premiums for the poor	2.1
60	Increased cash transfers (LEAP)	1.6
62	Diesel microgrids for more remote communities	1.8
63	Reduced LPG tax for cooking	1.9
64	Reduced industrial electricity tariff	1.9
65	Storm drain widening	1.8
66	Rural community led total sanitation with latrine subsidies	1.7
67	Rural community led total sanitation	1.3
68	Formalize mining co-operatives	1.2
69	Increased microfinance	1.6
70	Free school uniforms for girls	2.9
71	Urban bus rapid transport system	1.5
72	Schizophrenia screening and treatment	1.6
73	Retention ponds in Accra	1.4
73	Home garden and poultry training	1.3
75	Localized solid waste management by community members	1.1
75	Social housing construction	1.0
77	Ferries and ports on Volta	1.2
78	State sponsored alumina industry	1.1
79	Special Economic Zones	<1

Commentary
by Mr Ken Ofori-Atta

Ghanaian economist and an investment banker and co-founder of Databank in Ghana. He currently serves as Ghana's Minister for Finance. He was appointed by President Nana Akufo-Addo on 10th January 2017. Mr. Ofori-Atta was the first African to be honoured as a Donaldson Fellow at Yale University in 2010, a John Jay Fellow at Columbia University in 2011 and also a Henry Crown Fellow of the Aspen Institute. He is a Co-Founder of the Aspen African Leadership Initiative. He received a BA in Economics from Columbia University in New York and an MBA from the Yale School of Management.

The set of BCRs presented by the researchers served as a useful guide and benchmark. The strength of the BCR was the possibility to compare a wide set of policy-proposals, reaching from land-title reform to improved tuberculosis treatment.

However, given the challenges posed by data limitations in many instances, and the non-inclusion/omission of some important considerations in the research framework of individual researchers, the rankings were also influenced by personal knowledge of the available literature, informed intuition, and the political economy for implementation success.

Nothing happens without revenue availability. Consequently, high priority was given to measures that have a broad positive contagion effect in improving revenue mobilisation at the local government level. This is why I rank digital property and fees as the best solution, because this policy secures increased revenue, thereby allowing Ghana to invest in more policies.

Health is critical. A healthy population, including that of the active workforce, is important for economic development. This is why I place incentive schemes for health workers in remote areas as the fifth best intervention, as this would improve the quality of health services in these regions.

Improvements are also to be made in rural areas, why I place ambulance maintenance as the seventh best intervention. The same holds for an educated population armed with the right skills and knowledge required to drive development in all the sectors in these modern times.

Doubling investments in research and development were also rated highly in the BCR, and I agree on this assessment, why this was rated the sixth best investment. Consequently, health and educational issues where accorded higher priorities, although in most measure the within-sector BCRs were recognised in the prioritisation.

Finally, notwithstanding the above peculiarities, the rankings were, on the whole, broadly informed by the BCRs that evolved for the various research findings.

This project will hopefully inform citizens and decision-makers alike in Ghana. This is hopefully the first step of many to make good decisions in order to realize Ghana's full potential.

Authored by Dr. Samuel Nii-Noi Ashong

Top 50 by Mr Ken Ofori-Atta

1	Digitized property and business fees
2	Management training for medium sized firms
3	Eliminate NHIS premiums for the poor
4	Management consultants for large manufacturers
5	Incentive schemes for health workers in remote areas
6	Doubled R&D spending
7	Ambulance maintenance in rural areas
8	Complementary feeding promotion
9	Breastfeeding promotion
10	Micronutrients and calcium in pregnancy
11	Universal malaria testing and health facility treatment
12	Logistics for faster and more accurate TB testing
13	Active TB case finding in high risk groups
14	TB patient education for adherence
15	Comprehensive faecal sludge treatment plants
16	Sludge to energy plants
17	Biogas to energy plants
18	Strengthen community health system (GEHIP)
19	Emergency obstetric and neonatal care (EmONC)
20	Health worker home visits for pregnant and newborn
21	Land titling program
22	Build warehouses to reduce post-harvest losses
23	Revamp irrigation schemes
24	Increase mechanization through tractor services
25	Extend fertilizer subsidies
26	Hybrid maize seed subsidies
27	OPV maize seed subsidies
28	Support weaker 1-3 graders with teaching assistants
29	Organize all 1-3 graders according to learning level
30	Expand school feeding
31	Anxiety disorders screening and treatment
32	Community dialogues on schooling & early marriage
33	Subsidize private senior high schools to increase seats
34	Raise and sustain coverage of malaria bed nets
35	Vocational education
36	Preventive malaria medicine for children in Guinea Savannah
37	Poverty graduation
38	Rural community led total sanitation with latrine subsidies
39	Electricity grid for more remote communities
40	Solar microgrids for more remote communities
41	Electricity grid for less remote communities
42	Subsidize urban toilet constructions
43	Enforcement by-laws and latrine subsidies in urban areas
44	Diesel microgrids for more remote communities
45	Credit reference bureau
46	Rural community led total sanitation
47	Formalize mining co-operatives
48	Mass screening and treatment of hypertension
49	Stabilization ponds for remote areas
50	Improved cookstoves promotion to reduce urban air pollution

COMMENTARY
BY PROF. KWESI BOTCHWEY

Executive Chairman of the African Development Policy Ownership Initiative and Professor of Practice in Development Economics at The Fletcher School of Law and Diplomacy of Tufts University. Prof. Botchwey was Ghana's Minister for Finance from 1982 to 1995. He received his secondary school education at the Presbyterian Boys' Senior High School in Ghana. He holds an LL.B. from the University of Ghana, a LL.M from Yale Law School, and a doctorate from the University of Michigan Law School. He taught at the University of Zambia, the University of Dar es Salaam in Tanzania, and the University of Ghana.

I ranked all the 79 interventions during the Ghana Priorities conference. Broadly speaking, my ranking was based primarily on the BCRs, as modified by what I would call my 'informed intuition', that is my experience and knowledge of what our priorities should be in spending that 'extra dollar' for the attainment, in the final analysis, of the SDGs.

My assumption is that the purpose of our exercise, is, in the end, not just to enrich the academic literature on development policy generally, but to provide a guide to policy makers here in making investment choices in the framework of our budgeting planning processes.

Thus, interventions that may not have had high BCRs, I ranked higher if in my view, as determined by that 'informed intuition' they were essential and in the long run would facilitate the attainment of our development objectives in that broader context. In any case, we all know the limitations of the BCR!

So, for instance my first in the ranking is 'Universal malaria testing and health facility treatment'. Although this was not the highest BCR ranking, my reprioritization was based on the fact that malaria happens to be the leading cause of death and morbidity in Ghana and therefore such prioritization would enable us harvest greater benefits for the country as compared to the BCR by itself suggests. On the other hand, although 'TB patient education for adherence' scored highest on BCR rankings, it is not the leading cause of death in Ghana, and I am not sure I fully agree with the benefits calculation in the BCR in any case.

In the same way, my 4th, 5th, 10th, 28th and 31st rankings, all in the health sector are ranked higher than the BCRs, because I believe that if our community health systems are improved and strengthened and our ambulance services well maintained in the rural areas and NHIS premiums eliminated for the poor, this will go a long way in increasing access and building solid health systems thereby solving most of the fundamental health and equity issues confronting us as a country.

My 2nd ranking is on Local revenue mobilization. I strongly believe that if property and business fees are digitized, it would go a long way to rake in much revenue for and thereby re-energize the District Assemblies and local authorities that are chronically starved of resources, including statutory transfers mandated by the Constitution which the persistently cash-strapped national treasury is unable to provide. My view is that the benefits are grossly underestimated in the BCR estimation.

My 6th ranking was also on 'Compulsory SRH education for high school boys' and girls'. Intensifying access to sexual and reproductive health education would help place a check on population and reduce the risks of population demands on state amenities. It also increases the awareness of sexually transmitted diseases and infection and inculcate healthy sexual habits. The negative impact of uncontrolled population growth includes; an increase in street children, increased poverty levels and poor sanitation, just to mention but a few.

I ranked 'Land titling program' 3rd as opposed to its 4th ranking using the BCR. Easier access to land for formal economic activity can help reduce poverty drastically. Access to land in Ghana remains a challenge not only to the poor but also investors and local authorities for development. Our land tenure database is very poor and needs urgent improvement.

My 7th, 8th, 9th, 11th, 12th and 13th ranking are all on Agriculture. If we are able to produce more than we consume as a country, we would save on what we import to supplement what we produce. Also, value addition to export products will earn us foreign exchange to boost our economy. Producing more than we can consume as a country would also help keep food prices low, improve good nutrition for the majority of the citizenry which would also go a long way to help curb a lot of health issues such as malnutrition. In this as well as the 'Land Titling program' ranking, I believe that the benefits calculation in the BCRs was underestimated.

I ranked 'Rural community led total sanitation' 15th and Urban Sanitation interventions 17th and 18th. This varies greatly from the BCR ranking of 67th, 30th and 38th respectively. Diarrhea and cholera are the fourth most common disease for all outpatients treated in health facilities according to the Ghana Health Service in 2016.

The global burden of disease also estimated there were more than 41 million cases of diarrhea and more than 7,000 deaths from the disease in 2017. I believe such interventions to curb the current unsanitary conditions plaguing the country would reduce associated health risks and improve the estimated burden of disease. This would rake in more benefits than estimated and ultimately increase the BCR.

I ranked nutrition interventions, 25th, 26th and 27th. While I recognize that as a country, rate of undernutrition in young children still remains unacceptably high, I believe that with improved Agriculture, better health systems and education, nutrition levels can be improved without government outlays.

Interventions on poverty had BCR rankings of 54th, 59th and 61st for poverty graduation, increased cash transfers (LEAP) and increased microfinance respectively. I ranked them 61st, 66th and 72nd respectively. All these interventions have been implemented in the country already and has done very little to reduce poverty and to reduce the inequality gap.

Urban bus rapid transport system and Ferries and ports on Volta were ranked 77th and 78th respectively. The fundamental issues confronting our transportation system in Ghana is traffic regulation. I believe a comprehensive intervention to address traffic regulation and strict enforcement of our traffic regulations would help us make enormous strides in this regard.

TOP 50 BY PROF. KWESI BOTCHWEY

1	Universal malaria testing and health facility treatment
2	Digitized property and business fees
3	Land titling program
4	Strengthen community health system (GEHIP)
5	Eliminate NHIS premiums for the poor
6	Compulsory SRH education for high school boys and girls
7	Extend fertilizer subsidies
8	Revamp irrigation schemes
9	Build warehouses to reduce post-harvest losses
10	Ambulance maintenance in rural areas
11	Hybrid maize seed subsidies
12	OPV maize seed subsidies
13	Increase mechanization through tractor services
14	TB patient education for adherence
15	Rural community led total sanitation
16	Conditional asset transfer for girls enrolled in school
17	Subsidize urban toilet constructions
18	Enforcement by-laws and latrine subsidies in urban areas
19	Management training for medium sized firms
20	Doubled R&D spending
21	Capital grants for micro enterprises
22	Vocational education
23	Reduced industrial electricity tariff
24	Credit reference bureau
25	Micronutrients and calcium in pregnancy
26	Complementary feeding promotion
27	Breastfeeding promotion
28	Health worker home visits for pregnant and newborn
29	Logistics for faster and more accurate TB testing
30	Incentive schemes for health workers in remote areas
31	Preventive malaria medicine for children in Guinea Savannah
32	Management consultants for large manufacturers
33	Support weaker 1-3 graders with teaching assistants
34	Organize all 1-3 graders according to learning level
35	Community dialogues on schooling & early marriage
36	Family planning for unmarried women
37	Emergency obstetric and neonatal care (EmONC)
38	Family planning for married women
39	Monitoring devices on trawl ships
40	Improved cookstoves promotion to reduce rural air pollution
41	Improved cookstoves promotion to reduce urban air pollution
42	Expanded rural LPG distribution for cooking
43	Reduced LPG tax for cooking
44	Electricity grid for less remote communities
45	Diesel microgrids for more remote communities
46	Solar microgrids for more remote communities
47	Electricity grid for more remote communities
48	Replacement of illegal gears
49	Fishing Licences and Aquaculture
50	Apprenticeships

COMMENTARY
BY PROF. FINN E. KYDLAND

Henley Professor of Economics at the University of California, Santa Barbara. He also holds the Richard P. Simmons Distinguished Professorship at the Tepper School of Business of Carnegie Mellon University, where he earned his Ph.D., and a part-time position at the Norwegian School of Economics (NHH). Kydland was a co-recipient of the 2004 Nobel Memorial Prize in Economics, with Edward C. Prescott, "for their contributions to dynamic macroeconomics: the time consistency of economic policy and the driving forces behind business cycles."

Benefit/cost ratios for some of the interventions considered by the Ghana priorities are truly phenomenal – incredibly low-cost, with the potential to avoid a lot of suffering and save thousands and thousands of lives.

My two top-ranked interventions involve testing for TB and malaria. Each cedi spent would provide benefits of between 150 and 200 cedis!

For both TB and malaria, three interventions were ranked for each, all with high BCRs. An interesting question is if there are "economies of scale," so to speak. Suppose one decides to go ahead with the two top-ranked interventions, would the BCRs for adding the other two interventions in the same project area then be significantly higher than the estimated BCRs when done one by one? If so, it would be an especially powerful argument for doing all three of TB as well as all three of malaria.

Participating in CCC rankings more than once, as I've done in recent years, in Bangladesh and in the province of Andhra Pradesh in India, develops familiarity with certain interventions that show up again and again. One of my favorites is "Micronutrients and calcium in pregnancy." When encouraged to ask questions of the presenters, I submitted the following two on that intervention:

In the Guatemala study by Hoddinott et al. on a similar intervention, researchers returned to the subjects 25+ years later. The average wages of those who had benefited from the intervention were almost 50% larger. You seem to use a corresponding figure of an 8% increase, attributed only to differences in birth weight. There's no mention of cognition. In sum, is it possible that you've understated the effect on human capital (productivity) by a significant margin, even with your discount rate as high as 8%?

Do you think Ghana as a nation would benefit from a population growing up with the improved cognitive abilities from the intervention, perhaps emanating in ways that are difficult to measure directly from wages, more like a positive externality that manifests itself in more than one way?

These were formulated as questions, but really were intended as my comments on that intervention, to signify that I really appreciate the combination of the positive effects described (on stunting, cognition…), but also the enhanced ability to accumulate human capital, that is, higher earning power throughout adult life. As a consequence, with its BCR of 18, I even have four interventions with higher BCRs ranked below it.

One of my favorite interventions in countries such as Bangladesh, India, and Ghana are maize and other crops developed as GMOs. In Andhra Pradesh, after noticing the absence of GMOs among interventions considered, I asked about it. The answer was, they're not legal, which I find unbelievably misguided. Bangladesh has been much smarter. After they developed one of their favorite staples, eggplant, as a GMO, the resulting output was so large they can't eat it all themselves. But that just means they have plenty also to export, in return for other goods the nation needs.

In the case of Ghana, after observing the absence of GMOs from the list of seeds considered, there wasn't the opportunity for me to establish if there's a legality issue as in India. In any case, I did submit the following question/comment:

You've evaluated OPV and hybrid maize seeds, but not GMOs (such as golden rice). Why not? According to 155 Nobel Laureates (led by Sir Richard Roberts), GMOs are perfectly safe and especially promising for developing countries, as a source of food and also, essentially, as a source of medicine. The diets of millions of children are deficient in Vitamin A, resulting in blindness at young ages and deaths in the hundreds of thousands. I know of course that organizations such as Greenpeace and their allies have been trying to scare people (which, evidently, generates huge donations for these organizations). How many millions of children need to die before it becomes a crime against humanity?

Before submitting this question, I ran it by Sir Richard, who supported it fully. I imagine that means, in addition to Sir Richard and me, at least 153 Nobel Laureates support the use of GMOs!

At the end of the prioritizing, I generally find it interesting to compare my own ranking with the overall ranking – are there any glaring discrepancies? This time, it's clear that the largest one pertains to the two family planning interventions. I ranked that for married women number 5 and that for unmarried number 6. (To determine the order of the two, I decided to trust the estimated BCRs, 34 and 29, respectively.)

In the overall panel, family planning for married women is ranked number 36 and for unmarried number 49. I regard family planning as extremely important, as it makes it easier for women to achieve their educational goals and qualify for gainful work. This makes it easier, from a household budget standpoint and otherwise, to raise healthy and well-educated children. It's good for the household. It's beneficial for the nation as a whole. I can only surmise that, for the ranking to end up so low, there's something Ghanaians are worried about that I, as a foreigner, don't understand, perhaps related to the legal system, perhaps cultural.

I have a discrepancy also in assessment of BCRs for improved cookstoves, although not nearly to the same extent as for family planning. I have the two ranked interventions, with BCRs of 8 and 9 depending on urban vs. rural, ranked at number 28 and 31, while the overall panel ranks them at number 41 and 55. That worry about air pollution in some parts of the world is less than one tends to see in developed nations is quite commonly reflectied in CCC rankings. Perhaps the need to eat is the overriding factor, obviously not an unreasonable concern, although one can argue with the exact trade-off between the food-vs-pollution concern. Moreover, locals may have reason, based on experience in analogous situations, to worry about how the cookstove intervention actually will work when put into practice, how readily the improved stoves will be adopted, and so on.

Finally, we have examples also of the reverse – examples in which the panel ranking is high in spite of very low BCRs. My favorite one is vocational education, ranked 17 in spite of a BCR of only 1.3. As a result, vocational education is ranked more highly than 16 interventions that have BCRs of 5 or higher! Now, it so happens that vocational education is a topic about which I know a thing or two, as it's common and successful in several European nations, including my home country Norway.

Norway uses a 2+2 system, whereby, after two years of junior high, one can continue on an academically oriented track (required, for example, if applying to a university) or switch to training to become an electrician or plumber or painter or several other trades, more or less still under the umbrella of the high school system.

Bottom line, this system increases significantly the probability that one will eventually find employment at which one is skilled. (Members of my extended family in Norway are examples for whom this system worked very well.) Thus, I'm sympathetic to its placement in the overall ranking. I have a suspicion that the estimated benefits are understated by a significant margin. Evidently, enough members of the panel have that same suspicion, resulting in the ranking of 17th.

Top 50 by Prof. Finn E. Kydland

1	Logistics for faster and more accurate TB testing
2	Universal malaria testing and health facility treatment
3	Strengthen community health system (GEHIP)
4	Complementary feeding promotion
5	Family planning for married women
6	Family planning for unmarried women
7	Raise and sustain coverage of malaria bed nets
8	TB patient education for adherence
9	Land titling program
10	Micronutrients and calcium in pregnancy
11	Active TB case finding in high risk groups
12	Health worker home visits for pregnant and newborn
13	Breastfeeding promotion
14	Ambulance maintenance in rural areas
15	Preventive malaria medicine for Guinea Savannah children
16	Organize all 1-3 graders according to learning level
17	Management training for medium sized firms
18	Incentive schemes for health workers in remote areas
19	Digitized property and business fees
20	Capital grants for micro enterprises
21	Emergency obstetric and neonatal care (EmONC)
22	Expand school feeding
23	Monitoring devices on trawl ships
24	Credit reference bureau
25	Community dialogues on schooling & early marriage

26	Subsidize urban toilet constructions
27	Enforce by-laws and latrine subsidies in urban areas
28	Improved cookstoves promotion to reduce urban pollution
29	Depression screening and treatment
30	Extend fertilizer subsidies
31	Improved cookstoves promotion to reduce rural air pollution
32	Sludge to energy plants
33	Stabilization ponds for remote areas
34	Replacement of illegal gears
35	Support weaker 1-3 graders with teaching assistants
36	Management consultants for large manufacturers
37	Electricity grid for less remote communities
38	Biogas to energy plants
39	Anxiety disorders screening and treatment
40	Free school uniforms for girls
41	Mass screening and treatment of hypertension
42	Conditional asset transfer for girls enrolled in school
43	Hybrid maize seed subsidies
44	Revamp rail network for rural transport
45	Feeder roads for rural transport
46	Expanded rural LPG distribution for cooking
47	Doubled R&D spending
48	Comprehensive faecal sludge treatment plants
49	Compulsory SRH education for high school boys and girls
50	Increase mechanization through tractor services

Commentary
by Prof. Augustin Fosu

Professor, Institute of Statistical, Social and Economic Research (ISSER), University of Ghana. He also holds a number of (honorary) appointments, including: Extraordinary Professor, Faculty of Economic and Management Sciences, University of Pretoria, South Africa; BWPI Research Associate, University of Manchester, UK; and CSAE Research Associate, University of Oxford, UK. His previous positions include: Deputy Director, UN University-WIDER, Finland (2006-2013); Senior Policy Advisor/Chief Economist, UN Economic Commission for Africa, Ethiopia (2004-2006); and Director of Research, African Economic Research Consortium, Kenya (1998-2004). He holds a PhD in Economics from Northwestern University, USA. He has published widely, with certain rankings listing him among 'top economists/authors' in Africa and globally.

To rank-order the various proposed projects, I first read a given proposal, and form an idea of its viability, that is, a conceptual evaluation represented by an implicit benefit-cost ratio (IBCR). Employing the IBCR, I assign a whole number 1-10, with 10 as best and 1 as least. In certain cases, the viability is also guided by the actual cost, especially if the project's direct cost is huge. This is because the budget for Ghana Priorities must, of course, be bounded. Hence, even if a project has a relatively high estimated benefit-cost ratio (BCR), it may indeed crowd out other potentially viable projects, due to its large cost.

Sustainability is yet another determinant of viability. If a project is not sustainable, then the possible culture of dependency toward the project could generate adverse implications following the project's termination, unless the impact is sufficiently persistent.

To rank-order the projects, I revisit the proposals in order to differentiate among them by assigning finer ratings within each broad rating category. The BCR provides useful guidance for this second step. It additionally serves as a basis for revising the placement in the broad categories in certain cases. Finally, based on these ratings, I rank-order all the proposed projects.

In many cases, the BCR provides a reasonable approximation for the IBCR. However, it may deviate from the IBCR, because often measurable (economic) benefits and costs, captured by BCR, may not reflect other costs or benefits that are practically difficult to estimate. But also, the benefits may accrue to recipients other than consumers. I illustrate several of these related issues below.

The recipient of the benefits is crucial. For instance, where benefits accrue in the form of profits, it is not clear as to who actually ends up benefiting: workers, or shareholders? If it is primarily the latter, then the benefit should be discounted significantly, given its tendency to exacerbate inequality, especially in a developing-country setting. Unfortunately, the BCR does not undertake this accounting, given the methodological difficulty. Yet, it is the consumer welfare that should be optimized. Hence, I do not rank highly some of the 'industrialization' projects with high BCRs where the benefits are in the form of profits.

A particularly critical issue is the potential transformative nature of a proposed project. For example, the 'digitized property and business fees' project is assigned a relatively low BCR, especially when compared with many of the health-related projects. Nonetheless, this project is likely to be economically transformative. It will likely foster the revenue autonomy required for attaining economically viable decentralization. Unfortunately, such decentralization is unlikely to be undertaken by the central government, as there is little political incentive, thus requiring an external impetus.

Nor could the BCR possibly capture the benefits that would be generated by such a local-revenue autonomy. Currently, for example, the central government funds nearly all public schools: from primary to tertiary. And he who pays the piper (the central government) gets the tune, with the supply of education then subject to political machinations!

The provision of schools under such a scenario becomes essentially a 'free' public good to localities, resulting in political rivalry across localities toward obtaining their respective 'fair' shares. The likely outcome is over-supply, while a binding budget constraint of the central government results in less quality.

In contrast, under conditions of local revenue autonomy, there could be sufficient cost-sharing, thus limiting the cross-locality political rivalry toward the public good. The 'free' public good would, then, be converted to a local public good, with cost implications for locality choice. Unfortunately, none of these potential economic benefits are or could be captured by the BCR, implying that the IBCR likely substantially exceeds the BCR.

Another example is 'family planning', for the married or otherwise. A major problem in developing countries, including Ghana, is that there tend to be too many dependents, a phenomenon that is growth-retarding, that is, until demographic transition is reached. Yet, the BCR is unlikely to capture this phenomenon. Furthermore, there is little incentive for the political process to engage in such a program.

Instead, the tendency for the central government to provide 'free' public goods would exacerbate this problem of not ensuring that parents produce the number of children whom they can afford to cater for. And, even if families wanted fewer children, they might lack the necessary information to make the optimal decision. Hence, the IBCR for 'family planning' should be much larger than its BCR. The 'community dialogues and schooling and early marriage' project is conceptually similar.

There is also the issue of economic externality. For example, the BCRs for 'biogas to energy plants' and 'sludge to energy plants' seem relatively small. However, they fail to include the negative economic externality of the generated waste; instead they capture only the value of the produced energy. The IBCR that includes this externality would be higher than the BCR. The 'subsidize urban toilet construction' project is similar.

In addition, complementarity can create a large deviation of BCR from IBCR. Consider, for instance, the 'extend fertilizer subsidy' and 'hybrid maize subsidies' projects, whose BCRs pre-suppose that increased production would find the necessary market (Say's

Law?). However, this is not a plausible assumption in remote areas. Hence, unless other complementary projects are undertaken to justify this assumption, the IBCR is actually lower than the BCR.

Indeed, providing 'vertically' complementary projects, such as storage and market infrastructure, could serve to reduce the risk of failure. Thus, such projects should be undertaken in the form of a 'package'.

In conclusion, while the (estimable) BCR is useful, it represents a first- or second-order approximation of the conceptually defensible implicit BCR (IBCR), which represents the true viability of a project, and thus forms a more accurate basis for project selection. It is, therefore, the IBCR that primarily formed the basis for my rank-ordering of the various proposed projects under Ghana Priorities.

Top 50 by Prof. Augustin Fosu

1	Digitized property and business fees
2	TB patient education for adherence
3	Logistics for faster and more accurate TB testing
4	Land titling program
5	Active TB case finding in high risk groups
6	Family planning for married women
7	Biogas to energy plants
8	Sludge to energy plants
9	Family planning for unmarried women
10	Community dialogues on schooling & early marriage
11	Strengthen community health system (GEHIP)
12	Raise and sustain coverage of malaria bed nets
13	Preventive malaria medicine for children in Guinea Savannah
14	Universal malaria testing and health facility treatment
15	Health worker home visits for pregnant and newborn
16	Apprenticeships
17	Vocational education
18	Ambulance maintenance in rural areas
19	Incentive schemes for health workers in remote areas
20	Depression screening and treatment
21	Monitoring devices on trawl ships
22	Improved cookstoves promotion to reduce rural air pollution
23	Improved cookstoves promotion to reduce urban air pollution
24	Emergency obstetric and neonatal care (EmONC)
25	Electricity grid for less remote communities
26	Anxiety disorders screening and treatment
27	Replacement of illegal gears
28	Organize all 1-3 graders according to learning level
29	Support weaker 1-3 graders with teaching assistants
30	Complementary feeding promotion
31	Breastfeeding promotion
32	Micronutrients and calcium in pregnancy
33	Enforcement by-laws and latrine subsidies in urban areas
34	Subsidize urban toilet constructions
35	Expand school feeding
36	Hybrid maize seed subsidies
37	Build warehouses to reduce post-harvest losses
38	Compulsory SRH education for high school boys and girls
39	Extend fertilizer subsidies
40	OPV maize seed subsidies
41	Expanded rural LPG distribution for cooking
42	Eliminate NHIS premiums for the poor
43	Mass screening and treatment of hypertension
44	Increase mechanization through tractor services
45	Free school uniforms for girls
46	Conditional asset transfer for girls enrolled in school
47	Poverty graduation
48	Increased cash transfers (LEAP)
49	Subsidize private senior high schools to increase seats
50	Credit reference bureau

COMMENTARY
BY PROF. ERNEST ARYEETEY

Secretary-General of the African Research Universities Alliance (ARUA) and a former Vice-Chancellor of the University of Ghana. Prior to his appointment as Vice-Chancellor, he was a Senior Fellow and Director of the Africa Growth Initiative at the Brookings Institution, Washington, D.C. He was also Director of the Institute of Statistical, Social and Economic Research (ISSER) of the University of Ghana, Legon for the period February 2003 – January 2010.

1. Preliminary Priorities

My initial ranking was as follows:

	Intervention	BCR	Rank
1	Complementary feeding promotion	36	8
2	Eliminate NHIS premiums for the poor	2.1	50
3	Micronutrients and calcium in pregnancy	18	16
4	Breastfeeding promotion	24	12
5	Incentive schemes for health workers in remote areas	21	13
6	Formalize mining co-operatives	1.2	73
7	Build warehouses to reduce post-harvest losses	1.8	53
8	Preventive malaria medicine for children in Guinea Savannah	14	17
9	Ambulance maintenance in rural areas	21	15
10	Apprenticeships	2.4	46
11	Doubled R&D spending	1.5	63
12	Poverty graduation	1.8	54
13	Land titling program	91	4
14	Revamp rail network for rural transport	1.5	62
15	Revamp irrigation schemes	1.5	65
16	Digitized property and business fees	10	19
17	Fishing Licences and Aquaculture	1.2	72
18	Raise and sustain coverage of malaria bed nets	44	5
19	Universal malaria testing and health facility treatment	133	3
20	Support weaker 1-3 graders with teaching assistants	6	26

The first step involved in the preliminary ranking was to cluster the interventions by sector/industry. The sectors used were (1) education, (2) Health and Nutrition, (3) Industrialization, (4) Agriculture, (5) Social Interventions, and (6) cross-cutting issues.

The second step was to rank within each sector in terms of (1) how the intervention can address the most pressing problems within the sector/industry (2) the coverage of the intervention in terms of the estimated number of beneficiaries (3) the sustainability or otherwise of the intervention given the current circumstances of Ghana, and (4) if the intervention provides solutions to multisectoral issues.

I gave priority to interventions that presented unique and reliable solutions to various issues in Ghana. Interventions that upscale existing interventions without providing clear solutions to existing challenges were not given high priority. Interventions with excessively high BCRs were flagged. It was noted that the assumptions for some of these interventions were not valid.

I repeated the approach for each intervention and gave it a rank, where 1=most important; 2=second most important etc. All interventions that were ranked 1 were ranked again using the criteria in the Second Step for the final ranking. The was repeated for those ranked 2, 3, etc. to obtain the final ranking.

2. Ranking after Presentations

My top 20 rankings after the presentations became as follows:

	Area	Intervention
1	Malaria	Universal testing and health facility treatment
2	Malaria	Raise and sustain coverage of bed nets
3	Health system: Maternal and Child	Strengthen community health system (GEHIP)
4	Revenue mobilization	Digitized property and business fees
5	Agriculture	Hybrid maize seed subsidies
6	Agriculture	Revamp irrigation schemes
7	Agriculture	Extend fertilizer subsidies
8	Agriculture	OPV maize seed subsidies
9	Education - SHS	Subsidize private senior high schools to increase seats
10	Tuberculosis (TB)	TB patient education for adherence
11	Tuberculosis (TB)	Logistics for faster, more accurate TB testing
12	Health system: Maternal and Child	Health worker home visits for pregnant and newborn
13	Health Access	Ambulance maintenance in rural areas
14	Health Access	Incentive schemes for health workers in remote areas
15	Malaria	Preventive malaria medicine for children in Guinea Savannah
16	Tuberculosis (TB)	Active TB case finding in high risk groups

17	Nutrition	Complementary feeding promotion
18	Nutrition	Breastfeeding promotion
19	Nutrition	Micronutrients and calcium in pregnancy
20	Industrialization	Doubled R&D spending

It is obvious that my ranking of the nutrition interventions went down significantly after the presentations even though the BCRs were quite high. This was largely because I saw the agricultural and health interventions as presented to be more likely to generate greater impact than had been measured in the analysis. One of the health interventions that moved up significantly in the process was the intervention on universal malaria testing and health facility treatment with a BCR of 133.

It moved to the top of my list from the 19th position after listening to the researchers and the satisfactory answers to my questions on feasibility. Similarly, the interventions for TB with very high BCRs, had initially not featured much in my priority rankings because I considered them to be far less important than malaria.

I changed my mind and moved them up after the presentations because I realized that the benefits could be far more than I had previously believed.

The Land Titling intervention with a BCR of 91 moved down in my rankings after the presentation because I realized that there were far too many cultural and political obstacles to effective land tenure security enhancement, and that a land titling project was not going to solve that.

The proposed project for "Digitized Property and Business Fees" with a BCR of 10 moved up significantly to 4th position from the 15th position largely because I saw it as very innovative and likely to have a major impact on national governance, well beyond what the proponents intended.

I am very satisfied with the way the Ghana Priorities Project has been organized and believe that the rankings are a good reflection of the consensus that we arrived at during the workshop.

TOP 50 BY PROF. ERNEST ARYEETEY

1	Universal malaria testing and health facility treatment
2	Raise and sustain coverage of malaria bed nets
3	Strengthen community health system (GEHIP)
4	Digitized property and business fees
5	Hybrid maize seed subsidies
6	Revamp irrigation schemes
7	Extend fertilizer subsidies
8	OPV maize seed subsidies
9	Subsidize private senior high schools to increase seats
10	TB patient education for adherence
11	Logistics for faster and more accurate TB testing
12	Health worker home visits for pregnant and newborn
13	Ambulance maintenance in rural areas
14	Incentive schemes for health workers in remote areas
15	Preventive malaria medicine for children in Guinea Savannah
16	Active TB case finding in high risk groups
17	Complementary feeding promotion
18	Breastfeeding promotion
19	Micronutrients and calcium in pregnancy
20	Doubled R&D spending
21	Build warehouses to reduce post-harvest losses
22	Increase mechanization through tractor services
23	Monitoring devices on trawl ships
24	Electricity grid for less remote communities
25	Electricity grid for more remote communities
26	Replacement of illegal gears
27	Organize all 1-3 graders according to learning level
28	Support weaker 1-3 graders with teaching assistants
29	Expand school feeding
30	Fishing Licences and Aquaculture
31	Apprenticeships
32	Vocational education
33	Land titling program
34	Comprehensive faecal sludge treatment plants
35	Stabilization ponds for remote areas
36	Management consultants for large manufacturers
37	Management training for medium sized firms
38	Capital grants for micro enterprises
39	Reduced industrial electricity tariff
40	Revamp rail network for rural transport
41	Feeder roads for rural transport
42	Credit reference bureau
43	Diesel microgrids for more remote communities
44	Solar microgrids for more remote communities
45	Family planning for married women
46	Family planning for unmarried women
47	Expanded rural LPG distribution for cooking
48	Reduced LPG tax for cooking
49	Improved cookstoves promotion to reduce rural air pollution
50	Improved cookstoves promotion to reduce urban air pollution

Commentary
by Prof. George Gyan Baffour

Ghanaian development economist and politician. He is a member of the New Patriotic Party and the former Minister of Planning in Ghana. He was a professor at Howard University in Washington, D.C., from 1993 to 2001. He has a post-doctoral diploma from Harvard University, and obtained his masters and PhD at University of Wisconsin, Madison. He graduated with a BA in Economics from the University of Ghana, and proceeded to obtain a Diploma in Economics at the Helsinki School of Economics in Finland.

The Ghana Priorities ranking was based strictly in the arithmetic results of the Cost-Benefit Analysis, which technically is the best process as it ensures "value for money". However, as all the relevant data on each of the policies cannot be mustered there is always an allowance for reviewing based upon additional information and also the pertaining socio-economic circumstance at any given time.

My ranking is particularly influenced by the effect of the COVID-19 pandemic, which is very widespread and affecting every segment and the economy, lives and livelihoods in Ghana. The effort and development emphasis has thus been on the response, the recovery and the development of resilience towards similar situations in the future.

Policies that would have received immediate and high-level benefit rating just some six months ago are considered differently now in terms of economic benefits and live saving elements. The economic downturn where income in the private sector has reduced by 77 percent and nearly Ghc 7 billion short fall loss in revenue and additional Ghc 11 billion required to stabilize the economy and respond to pressing social protection and live saving interventions.

Significantly therefore my prioritization is influenced by the ability of the intervention to facilitate the response and recovery of the country under the COVID-19 effect. Much as a number of health and social responses have been scores very high under the CBA, and I agreed with a number of within the top twenty priorities to save live within the least cost, the sustainability of the intervention depends on the economic strength of the economy and the recovered status under the current situation.

I also observed the health and social interventions have direct link to life and therefore with the monetary estimates for life such benefits are easily assessed and accounted for which many of the other interventions yield indirect benefits accounted for by data and information which are not readily available. In addition to these observations, the research reports and the presentation revealed that there are challenges with data and information and thus the benefit and data streams and not fully covered. Some of these interventions included "Revamp rail network for rural transport", "Special economic zones" "hybrid maize subsidies "and "Extend fertilizer subsidies".

I ranked the generally direct economic, infrastructure and industrialization interventions with positive benefits high and at the top because they provide a fundamental development system upon which the other interventions will be sustained and complimented. My lowest rankings are on those interventions which might require more information to make the score reliable and also those other social interventions which seem to have been well covered by highly scored alternative interventions.

I also agree that high positive benefits indicate a worthwhile intervention and about 90 percent of the interventions are in the positive direction. The prioritizations on my part takes into consideration the complementary effect, the output-input linkages for some of them and the timing which, places additional premium or cost on the intervention. The combination of "land titling program" and "Digitized property and business" would drastically change productions systems and public revenue mobilization.

Investments in education is also a life changing intervention and therefore the high positive benefits score for "Expand school feeding", "support for weaker 1-3 graders…", "Organise all 1-3 graders according to learning level" as well as "Apprenticeship" and "Vocation".

Some of the infrastructure interventions are very vital for Ghana's intervention rendering even enormous indirection benefits through other sectors but the high investments cost involved makes the benefits margins just average.

The general observation is that the ranking of the proposals follows the general pattern of the of the CBA results with very few marked deviations including "Family planning for married women" and "Family planning for unmarried women". The observation is that there is a very strong positive correlation between women education and family planning the best approach is therefore to focus on the general education of girls and women, which provides for them knowledge, skills and ability to make informed choices. The last twenty interventions are all of the low CBA category, which is a good testimony for the process and results.

My conclusion is that the selected interventions largely represents the priorities of the country. The methodology is quite good there is however the challenge with data promptness to be able to make decisions relevant to pertaining times. The review by the panel thus fills this great gap and brings the results to reflect the current situation and indicate some of the gaps that are to be completed to authenticate the results.

The process and results present a great opportunity as NDPC is beginning the work of preparing for the next Medium-Term Development Plan (2022-2025). The priorities as reflected by the CBA and that of the other Eminent Economist will go a long to facilitate the review of the Coordinated Programme of the government, the SDG implementation process and more importantly the National Medium-Term Development Plan (2022-2025). It is my conviction that the result will have a great impact on the technical process of prioritizing and selecting programmes for financing under the national SDG initiative implemented by NDPC and MoP.

The Ghana Priorities process has finally established a reliable first step in selecting among national development interventions and the needed knowledge base must be established to particularly with the National Development Planning Commission to ensure the continuous application and relevance.

TOP 50 BY PROF. GEORGE GYAN BAFFOUR

1	Land titling program
2	Digitized property and business fees
3	Formalize mining co-operatives
4	Rural community led total sanitation with latrine subsidies
5	Feeder roads for rural transport
6	Extend fertilizer subsidies
7	Hybrid maize seed subsidies
8	Enforcement by-laws and latrine subsidies in urban areas
9	Revamp rail network for rural transport
10	Universal malaria testing and health facility treatment
11	Capital grants for micro enterprises
12	Management training for medium sized firms
13	Preventive malaria medicine for children in Guinea Savannah
14	Apprenticeships
15	Depression screening and treatment
16	Vocational education
17	Urban bus rapid transport system
18	Revamp irrigation schemes
19	OPV maize seed subsidies
20	Build warehouses to reduce post-harvest losses
21	Increase mechanization through tractor services
22	Biogas to energy plants
23	Strengthen community health system (GEHIP)
24	Breastfeeding promotion

25	Complementary feeding promotion
26	Home garden and poultry training
27	TB patient education for adherence
28	Electricity grid for more remote communities
29	Poverty graduation
30	Solar microgrids for more remote communities
31	Management consultants for large manufacturers
32	Fishing Licences and Aquaculture
33	Credit reference bureau
34	Reduced industrial electricity tariff
35	State sponsored alumina industry
36	Expanded rural LPG distribution for cooking
37	Increased cash transfers (LEAP)
38	Storm drain widening
39	Increased microfinance
40	Doubled R&D spending
41	Ambulance maintenance in rural areas
42	Incentive schemes for health workers in remote areas
43	Conditional asset transfer for girls enrolled in school
44	Organize all 1-3 graders according to learning level
45	Support weaker 1-3 graders with teaching assistants
46	Expand school feeding
47	Stabilization ponds for remote areas
48	Sludge to energy plants

49	Community dialogues on schooling & early marriage
50	Emergency obstetric and neo-natal care (EmONC)

COMMENTARY
BY PROF. EUGENIA AMPORFU

Associate Professor in the Department of Economics at Kwame Nkrumah University of Science and Technology (KNUST). She holds a PhD in Economics from Simon Fraser University, Burnaby, Canada, and she serves as an External Director on the Governing Board of the Bank of Ghana. She is a member of the Fiscal Council Ghana.

I have ranked all the interventions with the exception of those on Family Planning, to avoid conflict of interest. Please see below.

I ranked the health-related interventions above all the other because of the extensive impact on the health of the population. The first intervention on my list is 'Formalize mining cooperatives'. This had a BCR of 1.2 which appears low simply because the benefit, especially the reduction in exposure to mercury, focused only on the miners and ignored the exposure of the whole population to mercury. The mercury from illegal mining enters into water bodies, irrigating farms and hence entering into the food value chain. Thus, reduction in illegal mining reduces the health risk impact on at least part of the population and not just the miners.

The depression treatment intervention is efficient and since it takes side effect of treatment into account. However, counselling could have been included as a treatment without side effect.

I rank the first fourteen (14) intervention at the same level. These are Community dialogues on schooling & early marriage, Conditional asset transfer for girls enrolled in school, Anxiety disorders screening and treatment, universal malarial testing and health facility treatment, strengthen community health system, TB patient education for adherence, Active TB case finding in high risk groups, depression screening and treatment, micronutrients and calcium in pregnancy, logistics for faster and more accurate TB testing, Breastfeeding promotion, Complementary feeding promotion, and Poverty graduation.

I would also rank the next fifteen interventions at the second level. These interventions are: Apprenticeships, Vocational education, doubled R&D spending, Electricity grid for less remote communities, Localized solid waste management by community members, Retention ponds in Accra, Enforcement by-laws and latrine subsidies in urban areas, Revamp rail network for rural transport, Increased cash transfers (LEAP), Mass screening and treatment of hypertension, Reduced LPG tax for cooking, Solar microgrids for more remote communities, Improved cookstoves promotion to reduce urban air pollution, and Expanded rural LPG distribution for cooking.

These I rank as the next most beneficial interventions. Again, I am ranking them higher even though their BCRs are low, I think that the benefits in many of the interventions were under estimated.

For example, the Apprenticeship and the Vocational education interventions did not include the psychological benefits as well as social (status) benefits to participants. The doubled R&D spending is extremely important and further investigation is needed to explain the low BCR. Meanwhile I have ranked it among those at the second level.

The electricity grid for less remote areas also overlooked the benefit to students in the communities. The presence of electricity makes it possible for them to study for long hours without suffering any health impact. School performance for example could improve. The Enforcement by-laws and latrine subsidies in urban areas also did not include the resulting increase in rents to landlords after the installation of latrines in their homes. Feeder roads and rail for rural transport also has much more benefit on the morbidity of the population, and even makes it unnecessary for health facilities to be constructed in many rural communities, hence reducing public health expenditure. but were not included.

Even though the Digitized property and business fees intervention is pertinent to the local governments and so was ranked high by my colleagues, I rank at the third level because the main source of revenue to the local government is property tax. Thus, the ability of the intervention to broaden the tax base and increase funds to the local governments depends on land valuation which is closely related to the land titling intervention. Given that the land titling intervention is incomplete I would propose that at least, the lands and properties relevant to the MMDAs be surveyed and valued for the data collection purposes.

Land titling is also related to access to land and agriculture. I therefore rank land titling interventions together with all the agricultural interventions which is likely to have a higher BCR if integrated due to the complementarity of the interventions. I would rank these at the same level as the interventions for industry as well as education which is likely to generate more benefits that shown in the study.

The following interventions are ranked at the fourth level. These are schizophrenia, screening and treatment, raise and sustain coverage of malaria bed nets, fishing licenses and aquaculture, storm drain widening, compulsory SRH education for high school boys and girls, revamp irrigation schemes, extend fertilizer subsidies, rural community led total sanitation with latrine subsidies, expand school feeding, OPV maize seed subsidies, improved cookstoves promotion to reduce rural air pollution to reduce rural pollution, ambulance maintenance in rural areas.

These are all essential interventions however; the studies omitted some relevant parameters that are likely to affect their viability. For example, the ambulance maintenance intervention omitted the need for a supplementary vehicle, fertilizer intervention omitted environmental cost; and the raise and sustain malaria bed nets was too optimistic with patronage, and fishing licenses and aquaculture omitted the quality of the product.

I rank the remaining interventions at the fourth level because they are not expected to yield high returns. The ferry and ports on the Volta lake intervention would have a better yield if the intervention were on a multi-modal transport system that links the seaport and the airport to the communities along the lake. This would require the good network of water, rail and road transport system that could enhance tourism and businesses as well.

The intervention on the elimination of NHIS premium for the poor is more costly that appears in the study because identification of the poor in a largely informal sector economy require a lot of resources; preventive malaria medicine for children exposes the children health to the possible side effect of the medicine, the incentive schemes for health workers in the remote areas is too costly and is likely to attract doctors for only short periods. Increased microfinance intervention does not show good mechanism for borrowers to pay back the loans. Home garden and poultry training does not encourage specialization and trading.

Overall, these are very useful interventions and their conception and analysis required a lot effort. I congratulate all who were involved in bringing the work thus far.

TOP 50 BY PROF. EUGENIA AMPORFU

1	Formalize mining co-operatives
2	Community dialogues on schooling & early marriage
3	Conditional asset transfer for girls enrolled in school
4	Anxiety disorders screening and treatment
5	Universal malaria testing and health facility treatment
6	Strengthen community health system (GEHIP)
7	TB patient education for adherence
8	Active TB case finding in high risk groups
9	Poverty graduation
10	Depression screening and treatment
11	Micronutrients and calcium in pregnancy
12	Logistics for faster and more accurate TB testing
13	Breastfeeding promotion
14	Complementary feeding promotion
15	Apprenticeships
16	Vocational education
17	Doubled R&D spending
18	Electricity grid for less remote communities
19	Localized solid waste management by community members
20	Retention ponds in Accra
21	Enforcement by-laws and latrine subsidies in urban areas
22	Revamp rail network for rural transport
23	Feeder roads for rural transport
24	Increased cash transfers (LEAP)
25	Mass screening and treatment of hypertension
26	Reduced LPG tax for cooking
27	Solar microgrids for more remote communities
28	Improved cookstoves promotion to reduce urban air pollution
29	Expanded rural LPG distribution for cooking
30	Digitized property and business fees
31	Land titling program
32	Comprehensive faecal sludge treatment plants
33	Hybrid maize seed subsidies
34	Family planning for married women
35	Monitoring devices on trawl ships
36	Build warehouses to reduce post-harvest losses
37	Increase mechanization through tractor services
38	Support weaker 1-3 graders with teaching assistants
39	Subsidize private senior high schools to increase seats
40	Replacement of illegal gears
41	Management consultants for large manufacturers
42	Management training for medium sized firms
43	Credit reference bureau
44	Schizophrenia screening and treatment
45	Raise and sustain coverage of malaria bed nets
46	Organize all 1-3 graders according to learning level
47	Fishing Licences and Aquaculture
48	Storm drain widening
49	Compulsory SRH education for high school boys and girls
50	Revamp irrigation schemes

How these insights are implemented

The output of Ghana Priorities presented in this book provide food for thought, and a valuable policy-making input. The aim of the project is naturally to make a real impact on the lives of all Ghanaians, which we've luckily already seen happening.

The first success of Ghana Priorities came just over a month after the Eminent Panel. The top outcome was sponsored by the German GIZ and they were of course very excited that their project on digital revenue collection in Ghana's municipalities came in first. Their contribution was through the implementation of a software called District Local Revenue (dlRev), will ensure a faster data collection process, improved efficiency and increased revenue for the municipalities which they can use to provide better services to their constituents.

In late October, the Minister of Local Government and Rural Development, Hajia Alima Mahama, launched the "automated digital revenue management solutions" program based on the dlRev software. Because it had been named as the best solution for Ghana, it was an easy sell even just before the election, and GIZ and the local partner emphasized why such an investment was the right one for Ghana, with explicit references to the Eminent Panel ranking.

Other interventions are hopefully on their way. This is entirely likely, as the Directors of the Policy Planning Monitoring and Evaluation Directorates (PPMEDs) from all 18 ministries in Ghana have been presented with a prioritized list of 79 policy interventions for the country's future development.

Dr. Ralph Nordjo, manager of the Ghana Priorities project, and Dr. Felix Addo-Yobo, Director, Development Policy at NDPC, shared the findings from the panel of eminent economists at the NDPC's headquarters in Accra. The objective, in addition to the formal handover of the research and the prioritized results, was to discuss how to capture some of the policy interventions into the 2021 Budget.

Next, we've had a very close relationship with the National Development Planning Commission and its Director General, Dr. Kodjo Mensah Abrampha. All of the papers have been vetted, commented and co-published by the NDPC, leading to higher institutional awareness of the value of cost-benefit analysis. Dr. Abrampha has been extremely vocal in his support of the project leading to the NDPC to decide to use the cost-benefit approach in its analysis of the government's new policies over the coming years.

This could be the biggest, direct impact of the Ghana Priorities, as it will inevitably lead to systematically better, and better vetted policies. As NDPC also organizes all levels of government, the knowledge gathered and the approach will also be able to flow into the sub-national and local levels, as exemplifies in the digital revenue collection impact from above.

The importance of our close cooperation with the NDPC became all the more valuable in light of the pandemic.

As corona postponed the project conclusion from May to September, it also meant a very small window of opportunity to project the results before the country was consumed with its December election. The re-election of the current government but with a very small majority in Parliament leads to some very significant opportunities that we will continue to pursue in 2021.

First, the Budget Committee of the parliament has expressed strong interest in being presented with the prioritization and the research in more detail. This which comes from both political factions of the committee. Inspiring these politicians to champion more effective programs could have an outsized impact for the future of Ghana.

Next, we are currently publicising the top top-ranked solutions with the relevant, individual ministries and their top experts, in an article series on the top solutions co-authored by leading sector experts. This book represents in itself an effort to provide information to thought-leaders, policy advisors, and decision makers, but also students, sector experts, development professionals and the interested public. We will continue our partnership with NDPC. The EU has expressed significant interest in using the benefit-cost research and priorities to inform their new 7-year plan for Ghana.

This project was a trail-blazer for Africa, and was heard around the continent, both through its analysis on Covid and the Economist article. Although the impact on Ghana has always been the main focus of this project, many countries have signalled that they have found the results intriguing and are interested in something for their country. We're now working with Malawi and their National Planning Commission, and both of the heads (of both Ghana's NDPC and Malawi's NPC) are reaching out to their colleagues across the continent.

But for this project to reap its full potential, it depends on you, the reader, to take these ideas and apply them in real life. One of the best endorsements of the project came from in the editorial of Ghana's leading newspaper, that urged the implementation of the ideas that you've been presented to throughout this book. We can only agree.

Daily Graphic
Thursday, December 17, 2020.

Editorial

Daily Graphic
EDITORIAL
Thursday, December 17, 2020

Prioritising our developmental needs: The way to go!

THE rationale for prioritising developmental needs is that development gaps are huge, while resources to address them are scarce.

Prioritising, therefore, ensures that we put our limited resources into strategic actions and the best use that will yield the best results.

It will further ensure that the country does not waste its scarce resources on pursuing programmes and projects that will not benefit the masses.

Two months ago, precisely on Friday, October 9, 2020, the National Development Planning Commission (NDPC) briefed officials of ministries, departments and agencies (MDAs) on priority areas where the country should spend its scarce resources.

For 18 months, the NDPC, together with the Institute of Social, Statistical and Economic Research (ISSER) of the University of Ghana (UG) and the international think tank, the Copenhagen Consensus, engaged and researched to find the key priority needs on which to spend Ghana's resources to enhance accelerated development.

Going through research materials, publications and policies, the commission prioritised developmental areas on which the scarce resources could be put to great use.

A bipartisan group of eminent persons was also engaged to whittle down all the pressing developmental needs of the country to 19, saying if funds were committed to those areas, it would bring the utmost good to all.

The partners, after collating all the information, shared it with the MDAs for them to wisely apply their scarce resources to priority needs in all their activities.

Digitised property and business fees were identified as the first priority proposal, while the second was universal malaria testing and health facility treatment, with the strengthening of community health systems and the land titling programme being the third and fourth priority areas, respectively.

TB patient education for adherence to basic protocols was the fifth priority; logistics for faster and more accurate testing was the sixth, while logistics for accurate TB testing, ambulance maintenance in rural areas, preventive malaria testing for children in the Guinea Savanna and complementary feeding came in respectively.

Interestingly, the prioritised areas impact directly on citizens' health, and that is to be expected, as a healthy people are the country's most beneficial resource.

The MDAs are, therefore, to take the priority areas into consideration in their work, with the NDPC indicating at the briefing that competing needs meant pruning down to the most urgent, hence the 19 identified areas.

Some of the materials, which present the cost-benefit analysis of devoting funds for simple acts, such as TB education to ensure adherence, show that the benefits far outweigh the initial committed funds used in education.

The *Daily Graphic* believes that such home-grown analysis by the NDPC, the ISSER and the Copenhagen Consensus is important and the knowledge and products shared are the right ways to go if we are to have value for our money.

We urge that the NDPC monitors and ensures that MDAs focus on the priority areas identified.

Targets must be set and progress noted, so that Ghana, in small but sustained steady steps, reaches its goal of development.

In the midst of resource constraints, how do we prioritise needs for development?

Nyamekye Amoako

Our needs, such as food, potable water, accommodation and

Adonu Raphael

The government must invest heavily in vocational education and make it more attractive. Students

R. K. Sarpong

We must strengthen our human resource capacity by improving our educational systems to align with our

Made in the USA
Monee, IL
12 November 2026

61d4ea2a-96a0-46cd-abcb-3258317f7e80R02